Conquer Your Fears In 30 Hours

By Maxwell S. Cagan

SUNVILLAGE
publications

www.sunvillagepublications.com

Conquer Your Fears In 30 Hours
By Maxwell S. Cagan

Copyright © 2010

www.sunvillagepublications.com

Cover photography by Eric Grevaert
Cover design by www.WebCopyAlchemy.com

For more powerful self-help techniques
and mind-tools visit us online at:
www.MindPowerSelfHelp.com

To my wife BETTY

who encouraged me from the start

and stood by all the way

this book is fondly dedicated

CONTENTS

Contents

Contents

LIFE DOES NOT always run smoothly and many a step taken with the best intentions in the world does not turn out as well as expected. Even under ideal conditions, in the midst of our modern social and economic system, we are faced with problems day after day that call for specific decisions. Some of them involve only minor adjustments, others necessitate drastic changes or complete reversals in habitual behavior. But whatever the need our feelings or emotions of the moment definitely influence our actions and greatly affect our final decisions.

To be able to meet conditions as they arise one must be prepared for them. But unfortunately many an individual is handicapped from the start. Whether it be due to environment, to personal make-up, to conditioned reflexes, to preconceived notions, to lack of self-reliance or to emotional instability, many of us cannot face realistically the every-day problems of life.

We look for a way out and seek to escape the pending changes or the new responsibilities. We try to ignore them, to submerge or to suppress them, and that often marks the beginning of a complex or a neurosis.

The Chinese are great believers in preventive medicine and we, too, may find it advantageous in days to come to utilize the vast resources of modern medical science and mental therapy to keep us physically, mentally and emotionally fit at all times.

This book has two main objectives. 1st. To reach those who are advancing in years and are gradually growing tense, discouraged, easily upset or emotionally disturbed without knowing why. 2nd. Those who are already beset by fears, worries, anxieties, frustrations or mysterious ailments and want to help themselves.

If you belong to the first group this book may help you arrest and prevent emotional disturbances. If you belong to the second it may start you looking for the underlying causes and help you find ways to eliminate them.

But to do any of these things effectively you must "pin-point" the contributory factors, and the way to start is to ask questions of yourself. For instance, why do you think that no one needs you, wants you or is in any way concerned about you? Why are you beset by fears and anxieties which you cannot explain? Why do you feel insecure even in the midst of your immediate family? Why are you troubled by mysterious aches and pains which defy usual medications? Why do you consider yourself inferior or subservient to others?

Do inner conflicts keep you on edge? Do you nurture grudges, resentments or animosities without cause? Are you lonely most of the time? Do you find yourself unable to make or retain friends? Do you feel uncomfortable in the midst of people and would rather be alone? Do you suffer from a feeling of guilt? Are you caught in a grip of misery, of compulsions or obsessions, and see no way out? Have you lost your mate recently and in the midst of your grief feel that life is no longer worth living?

Do you think of yourself as a misfit or a failure? Are you now retired but fail to enjoy your leisure hours? Have you become estranged from God and the spiritual uplift of prayer? Do you feel you could still be useful to others and to yourself if only you were shown how and given the chance?

If any of those questions apply to you then this thirty-day guide to happier living can help you, no matter what your age, your sex, your background or your economic status might be.

This guide will show you how to analyze yourself, how to evaluate your promptings and potentials, how to minimize objectionable traits, how to meet minor problems, how to banish fear and worries, how to adjust yourself to the inevitable, how to regain spiritual faith, how to find outlets for self-expression, how to rebuild self-confidence, how to develop new interests, how to make friends, and how to get more out of life within the framework of your present age, standing, background and environment.

But none of these projected objectives can be reached by you unless you are sincere in your desire to help yourself and work conscientiously at it. However, do not consider this book as the cure-all for all emotional disturbances, as a panacea for all ills or maladjustments or as a magic carpet that will take you to a land of joy, happiness and contentment.

The ideas given cannot transform you into a totally new personality in one day or in thirty days. They cannot eradicate the mistakes of the past, discard the effect of bad habits, ignore the restrictions of your age, discount the limitations of your background or disregard your physical condition. Some of them will have to remain as they are, although improvements can be made.

The material given is intended to show you the way. The simplified, intimate talks are meant to serve as steps leading upward to a richer, fuller, better and happier life. The order of their presentation is not indicative of their importance or relationship. Some are only informatory or explanatory in content and others are specific in their suggestions.

Use them as they apply to your wants and problems. If any of the talks apply specifically to you make them your pivotal point of contact. Combine them with others closely related to the same topic and let them become the center of your activity until the situation is changed and your problem is resolved. Then go on to the next step in your steady climb upward. What is more, if the material given is not enough for your purposes follow it up by further studies through your local library. Your librarian can help you in many ways to supplement a follow-through.

Use this procedure right along and you will benefit immeasurably by it. It will help you to gain a better understanding of yourself, to develop a healthier outlook upon life, to broaden your horizons, to discover newer and better ways for self-expression. It will encourage you to cultivate new friends and enrich your contacts with them. It will foster within you a sense of security, a feeling of pride and accomplishment, the knowledge that you belong and are an integral part of life around you. That, in turn, will engender within you peace, well-being and contentment.

Thus, in a figurative sense, this book will start you climbing, day by day, step by step and hour after hour, on an imaginary stairway upward. Each tread in that stairway will bring you closer to the uppermost balcony where the view is glorious, beautiful and unlimited. Each riser in that stairway will introduce you to new concepts, to new vistas and horizons. Each step upward will contribute its share toward your ultimate goal, to richer, fuller, better and happier days. In fact, these stairs would become your own private stairway to success and happiness, only thirty space hours away.

Los Angeles, California   MAXWELL S. CAGAN

The First Hour

WHO AND WHAT ARE YOU?

THIS IS the first hour in the first day of your thirty day climb to revitalize your mental outlook, to eliminate harmful habits, to reduce your fears and to gain a better hold upon your feelings and emotions. Mark this moment well. Engrave it upon the tablets of your memory. It is the beginning of a new, bright, glorious future for you, the sure way to happier days.

Hour after hour, in simple easy-to-climb steps, one riser at a time, for the next thirty days, you will be climbing slowly, surely, continually upward. Day by day, as you mount another step and leave part of your old, drab, dreary past below, you will gain in knowledge, in perspective, in self-understanding. Day by day, as you add to your vantage points, widen your horizons, enlarge your concepts, reduce inner conflicts, learn to make new friends and strengthen your hold upon inner disturbances you will discover new depths and new potentialities within you. You will, then, be able to reshape your little world and develop a new and more desirable personality.

Be sure to follow through or else the new heights you aim for will not bring you all the benefits desired. Each step upward may call for a modification in your thinking, in your outlook or in your behavior, but such changes will be fairly easy to make.

You will be climbing only one step at a time and only one change or modification will be required. And, it will be not so much the particular value of any given step or single change as the accumulated effect of a number of them that will bring you eventually to the top.

So—be patient in your quest for fuller, richer and happier days. Do not skip a single step upward. Do not hurry to reach the first or the subsequent landings on the way to the top. Give yourself time to get used to the new heights and the new concepts. Take a full day's breathing spell after each step and between climbs. Let your new perspectives become an integral part of your mental outlook before you add more to them.

Renew your efforts every day to get ahead, to gain self-control, self-confidence and self-understanding. Make each day's reading the important assignment for that day. Read and reread each paragraph and give yourself time to digest and absorb its contents, and if some particular passage strikes you or applies specifically to your needs underline it. Then go over it again and again until it becomes part of you and gives you the lift and the encouragement you need.

Then, and only then, will this book become your personal guide upward. Then, and only then, will you become better equipped to study yourself. Then, and only then, will you begin to look inwardly, to evaluate your promptings, to probe into your problems, to understand the reasons for your disturbances and thus learn how to gradually eliminate many of your fears, anxieties, worries and frustrations.

You will also learn, at the same time, that deep within you are many undiscovered and undeveloped potentialities. They may well be immortal sparks of greatness lying dormant within you that can be kindled into glowing fires of tremendous value.

You are the sun and the moon and the stars in your own private universe and you can make them shine and gleam and glisten in the beauty of your life, in the wisdom of God and in the happiness of your days.

This is the beginning of a new life for you and you have already taken the first step forward and upward at this very moment. It is in your awareness that there are disturbing factors in your present emotional make-up. It is in your desire to look for the contributory causes and try to eliminate them. It is in your reading these lines and in your willingness to follow through in the projected thirty-day plan. It is in your readiness to study, to learn and to use the ideas suggested to the best of your ability.

Begin by evaluating yourself and realizing that you are something unique in this world of ours. All of man's inventions and discoveries are as nothing compared to the intricate, infallible, automatic mechanisms which are you and which you take for granted.

You are the most amazing and mystifying combination of complicated, interrelated systems of communications, transportation, transformation, operation, circulation, coordination, elimination and various processing plants ever brought together into one organism.

Within you, visible and invisible to the eye, are literally dozens of automatic independent, self-managing, self-cooperating, self-regenerating units working silently, smoothly, efficiently together to keep you in perfect condition. Each unit is entrusted with certain chores. Each has its specific, separate, distinct, particular tasks, limits, purposes and areas of operation. Yet they are so delicately attuned one to the other, so smoothly dovetailed in their overlapping activities, so perfectly coordinated in their respective fields in an incessant round-the-clock lifetime activity as to defy human duplication.

For instance, your body contains about seven quarts of blood, yet your heart pumps over eight thousand quarts or better than one thousand times that amount of blood through your system during every day of your life. Your heart valves open and close, under normal conditions, seventy times a minute, or about one hundred thousand times a day. Multiply it by the number of days in your present age and the astronomical figures will amaze you. Can you think of any pumping system devised by man to equal that heart of yours?

Or consider your blood circulation. To reach the millions of body cells your blood has to cover a route from 60,000 to 100,000 miles long and on its way adapt itself instantly to the different sizes and capacities of every vein, artery and capillary in your body. Some of your blood vessels are only 1/2 50th of an inch in diameter and your blood corpuscles can enter and leave only one at a time. Yet your blood does this herculean task steadily, smoothly, silently, perfectly, and delivers the exact flow of blood needed by each tissue and organ, every time and all the time.

In addition to its delivery tasks your blood has other important duties and for such purposes maintains two huge armies. The first is comprised of trillions of red corpuscles. A trillion is the numeral one followed by twelve zeros. These corpuscles bring oxygen, amino acids, vitamins and minerals to every nerve and cell in your body and on the return trip carry back the carbon dioxide with the other wastes and poisons which have to be discarded.

The second army, the trillions of white corpuscles, the leucocytes, police your entire system once every twenty-eight seconds. Their job is to attack and destroy invading germs, microbes, or bacteria, brought in by filth, dirt, dust, poisons, injury or contamination. They do their task incessantly, automatically, whether you are awake or asleep, as long as they remain in a healthy condition to fight and have not been weakened by an anemic condition, by prolonged sickness or by wanton excesses.

Or consider your memory. To duplicate even in a minor way its storage capacity it would take several Congressional libraries, floor after floor of filing cabinets and hundreds of trained librarians just to gather, to separate, to index and to classify the millions of images, incidents, impressions, experiences and flashes of identification which you have collected through the years and which you can recall at will in fractions of a second.

These are but three of the God-given highly complicated systems which are yours to use and to benefit by, at a moment's notice. They are marvels of complicated ingenuity, and yet you take them as a matter of course and give them a second thought only when something happens to interfere with their perfections.

To continue the evaluation of you, it might interest you to know that there is no one like you in the whole world. As a human being and as a member of the male or female branch of mankind you have your physical and organic counterpart in all the other human beings alive. Although you may differ from them in size, height, weight, build, age, color, race, nationality, background, traits, habits, environment and living standards, basically you are very much like all the other persons on this planet.

However, when we begin to compare, consider and evaluate personality, sensitivity, receptivity, mentality, adaptability, intelligence quotients and potentialities, marked differences appear not only among people within the same general group or classification or among members of one family but even between identical twins. This is where you become a distinct individual, a separate little world all your own.

As a matter of record, and phylogeny as well as psychology substantiate it, no two individuals are exactly alike in every respect. In all the millions who lived before you, who are alive today and will be born in the future there never was and never will be anyone exactly like you. Nature and God have given you special talents, abilities and aptitudes, which only you can use and develop.

You have never fully utilized those talents of yours, for various reasons. You may have been too busy growing up, learning a trade, following a profession, raising a family, paying for a home or meeting your obligations, and therefore never gave all your potentialities much of a chance.

But what about now? Can you give ear to those hidden urges and let them find expression now? It is never too late and your present age can hardly be an obstacle.

Benjamin Franklin penned his autobiography after he was eighty years old. Tennyson wrote one of his greatest poems "Crossing the Bar" at eighty-three. Paderewski was giving highly popular piano concerts at eighty and Thomas Edison began new experiments with synthetic rubber substances at eighty-three.

Dr. Louis Perlman of New York City started studying medicine at fifty-eight and became a licensed physician at sixty-six. Albert Schweitzer did much of his notable work after the age of seventy. Grandma Moses began painting at seventy-four. Winston Churchill was nearing three score and ten when he took over the English ship of state and piloted it through years of strife and peril.

And on his eighty-second birthday former President Herbert Hoover had this advice for oldsters: "Keep busy at doing something, otherwise you will degenerate in talking to everybody about your pains and pills and income taxes . . . Even a part time job is worth a great deal . . . It adds meaning to life . . ."

So—take courage and follow through on the promptings of your heart. They were never meant to be stifled, ignored or forgotten. If you have the urge to sing, to write, to paint, to travel, to make things or to learn something entirely new to you, go ahead and do it—now. Your first attempts may be poor and discouraging but do not let it dismay you. Keep trying again and again for that in itself is an accomplishment.

You are nature's greatest achievement, the most amazing and most complex form of life on earth. You are man created in the image of God and you can reach the loftiest heights. So—raise your head on high and strive to do better each and every day as you climb onward and upward on your stairway to success and happiness, only twenty-nine space hours away.

The Second Hour

HOW MANY OF "YOU" ARE THERE?

WHETHER OR NOT you are aware of it, you are a composite being with several different "you's" in control, one overlapping the other. There are outer and inner "you's".

One of the outer "you's" is your body and its component parts, that are visible and invisible to the eye. This includes all the inner organs, the nervous system and everything else about you that can be located, isolated or identified. As a matter of fact, there is hardly any part of your physiological "you" which cannot be reached in some manner and which does not lend itself to check-up, analysis, diagnosis and treatment or correction when necessary.

The outer "you" is also represented by the sum total of your traits, mannerisms, characteristics and mode of behavior. It is the outward indication of your make-up, of who and what you appear to be. It is the impression others get of you as to your character, abilities and personality. It is the feeling you generate in others as a parent, a friend, a neighbor, a worker or associate.

The inner "you" is represented by your mental "you's". They

comprise the emotional, creative, imaginative, conscious, unconscious and the spiritual "you's", and are the most complex part about you.

They baffled man through the ages and to this day men of science and medicine still grope partially in the dark and still do not know what the complete mental "you" is. They know that the mind is the hub of all human activity, the control center for all thought, feeling, emotion and reaction. They have been able to identify the thalamus, and isolate portions of the brain which control various urges, senses, impulses and responses. But they have not learned as yet how and why we differ so much from each other in mental make-up, nor have they been able to find out why or what makes one person an average individual and another a mental genius.

Your mental "you" is what you make it. Barring basic functional deficiencies or physical impairments your brain can be trained and developed in numerous ways. It can grow, expand, project, deduce, combine, learn and remember. It can be directed into specialized channels and be conditioned to strange stimuli.

The creative "you" is that inner urge to find expression, recognition and self-fulfillment. Behind it are the dormant urges and potentialities within you that need only be tapped to open a new, glorious world of joy and satisfaction.

The imaginative "you" is the amazing ability of your mind to project itself into the unknown, the unexplored and the unexpected. It is in your capacity to dream, to envision new, entirely different and seemingly impossible ways to do things, to live and to make life more enjoyable.

The conscious "you" is the reasoning, analytical "you" which enables you to compare, contrast, deduce, evaluate and come to certain decisions. That, however, is governed by your emotions which are the motivating power behind your behavior, your actions and reactions. They, in turn, are controlled by habit and it is within your power to change your habits to suit.

The unconscious "you" is that vast, hidden, powerful force within you, as propounded originally by the father of psychiatry, Dr. Sigmund Freud.

He envisioned the unconscious as the repository of all dissatisfied urges and impulses, as the storehouse of all resentments, inhibitions, grievances and frustrations. He saw the primacy of sex as the motivating force in the unconscious, as the representative of repressed and ungratified amoral desires. He maintained that the unconscious never forgot and never forgave for those repressions and claimed that unless it was diverted, through sublimation or transference, into constructive channels, it always exacted a toll in mental derangements.

According to Freud's teachings those repressions grow into monsters within us. They lurk in the dim, dark recesses of our mind and are ever ready to pounce upon any opening or mental deviation. They prey constantly upon our thoughts, feelings and emotions, without us knowing it. Thus, they foster moods, build up resentments, engender frustrations and lead to complexes, fixations, neuroses and phobias. These promote psychosomatic ailments and when left unchecked lead to psychoses.

Freud maintained that our mental aspects were based upon the "id," the "ego" and the "super-ego".

He envisioned the "id" as the core of the unconscious, as the raw, primal, primitive, atavistic urges of man. To him, the "id" was a lusty, living thing within us, carnal, selfish, bestial and utterly relentless in its instinctual drives. He compared the "id" to an infant driven by basic powerful urges, by its need for ease and comfort, by its insatiable craving for love and attention, by fierce dominant jealousies, by the overwhelming desire to possess those it loved, by its refusal to share such love with others and by its want to dominate everything within reach or else destroy it so that others could not benefit.

Freud saw the "ego" as that part of our mental make-up which has to do with our thoughts, our actions and reactions. As he explained it, the ego has transference and sublimation at its disposal. It also has various escape and defense mechanisms to protect the individual from the selfish, sensual and often self-destructive demands of the "id".

He envisioned the "super-ego" as the moralistic part of our thought processes, as the fountainhead of our sense of duty, of loyalty, of fairness, of responsibility. The super-ego was, in his way of thinking, the seat of conscience and yet could not be tied in directly with the acquired sense of moral, social, ethical and religious taboos, obligations and restrictions.

Freud saw the id, the ego and the super-ego in constant conflict, one with the other, each trying to get the upper hand and upset the delicate balance. Their imbalance always brought maladjustments and they, in turn, usually led to some form of neurosis or psychosis.

Freud's preoccupation with sex was not shared by his early disciples, Alfred Adler and Carl Jung. His theories were also challenged, in the 1920s, by Otto Rank, by Sandor Ferenczi and by Wilhelm Reich. Then, in the 1930s, Karen Horney, Eric Fromm and H. S. Sullivan challenged the others and began stressing the social and cultural factors in neurosis and the interpersonal aspect of the analyst-patient relationship.

Freud's theories led to the system of psychoanalysis wherein the patient is encouraged to speak freely and openly of all the things which trouble him. He is urged to recall his childhood days, his early fears, anxieties, animosities, resentments and especially the surcharged emotional experiences and disappointments. Such open recitals expose his repressions to the light of the older and more matured mind. This often strips them of their influence or importance and serves to nullify their effect.

However, when such recollections are not sufficient in themselves, the psychiatrist may utilize other means to get at the mental block. For such purposes he may resort to shock treatments, to gland therapy, to methatol, to sodium pentathol or to carbon dioxide injections.

Many new ideas in approach, in analysis, in treatment and in technique have been developed within recent years to cope with mental aberrations. Yet Freud's original concepts are basically sound and because of his teachings thousands of mentally disturbed persons have been helped.

The spiritual "you" is that inner drive for oneness with God. It is the spark of divinity implanted within you at birth. It is the stirrings of the soul, the seat of goodness, of kindliness and loftiness. It is the spiritual affinity that always strives for all that is pure, fine, noble and elevating in man.

Capitalize upon all of these "you's" within you and above all listen to the promptings of your soul and harken to its message of truth. Then you will surely gain in peace, in serenity and in happiness as you continue to climb upward on your stairway to success and happiness, only twenty-eight space hours away.

The Third Hour

WHAT IS YOUR PHYSICAL CONDITION?

HAVE YOU HAD a physical check-up lately? Have you taken time out within the last year from work or from play, to consult a competent diagnostician and have him give you a thorough examination?

If not, do it now, because even a casual check-up may reveal certain conditions about your state of health that need attention or correction. This is true especially if you are past forty and have allowed yourself to drift along "as is" for the last few years.

You may be doing the wrong things and perhaps are shortening your span of life without knowing it. You may have the beginnings of a metabolic, arthritic, tumorous or a vascular system ailment that can be arrested or corrected before it gains headway and brings serious complications.

Let the doctor give you a complete and thorough examination, including X-rays, cardiograms and feces analysis. Then with the findings before him he will be ready to tell you exactly what is right or wrong for you. And, if you wish to reach a ripe healthy old age, free of complications, take your doctor's advice.

He will give you fundamental rules for diet, sleep, work, play and other activities. Those rules will be based upon your age, your medical history and your physical condition. Be sure to follow them and health will be yours to have and to enjoy.

Nothing is more important to your well-being than good health, and this is how Lawrence Sterne summed it up: "O blessed health! Thou art above all gold and treasure. 'Tis thou who enlargest the soul, openest all its powers to receive instructions and to relish its virtues. He that has thee has little more to wish for, and he that is so wretched as to want thee, wants everything with thee . . ."

A great deal has been said and taught about will power. But you may find it more effective to use a little "wont" power. When you feel inclined to overeat or imbibe or do something else you know you are not supposed to do, say to yourself "I wont do it!" and live up to it.

The greatest enemy to good health and well-being is self-indulgence in little things. If fried or highly seasoned foods are not good for you, indulging your appetite for them even on a small scale will be just as harmful for you. If smoking is bad for you, refuse to indulge even in one or two smokes. And, if playing handball is hard on your heart, confining it to one or two games a week will be just as harmful and may do you irreparable damage. Learn to use your "wont" power and refuse to gratify a small wish just because you are self-indulgent.

You cannot cheat on yourself and expect to be the winner. You cannot continue to abuse yourself, even in a small way, and not pay for it afterwards.

The important part to remember is that a physical illness or breakdown affects everything else about you. Your thoughts, your feelings and emotions and even your outlook on life is influenced and colored by your physical condition.

A person who does not feel well, who is beset by pain or incapacitated by sickness cannot be calm, composed and normal in his actions and reactions. He cannot be sociable, amiable or considerate as usual. He cannot weigh facts properly or evaluate anything in his customary manner. In fact, if there is too much pain or discomfort he cannot see or think straight. This definitely affects his general behavior and his relationships with others.

Guard your health and it will help you obtain and retain a saner, healthier outlook on life. It will also help you to be your natural, normal self. Too many of us like to look, to act and to appear important. We feel neglected when we are not the center of interest and at times will do most anything to draw the desired attention to ourselves.

How about you? How often do you brag and boast about the importance of your job, about your influential friends, about your past, about your activities in various groups or about other things that strike your fancy for the moment?

How often do you assume supercilious airs, convey the impression that you know all the answers, pretend you are too big to be bothered with petty things or make believe that money, as such, means nothing to you? How often do you seek recognition and would compromise yourself a dozen times, confidentially of course, to get a little publicity?

Have you ever stopped to ask yourself why you are so anxious to impress people? Psychologists say it is a form of anxiety and the basic reason for it lies in a feeling of inferiority. You want people to think that you are an important person. And so, you build the illusion around you that you have power, friends and influence. Yet, at the same time, anxiety stays with you. You are constantly afraid that someone might look behind your false front and see you for what you really are. . . . And, you begin to brag and boast a little bit more.

Titles, honors, badges of office, deference and prepaid servitudes have little meaning to the truly "big" man. He is above simple pretensions and petty subterfuges. He does not have to play a part or make believe, and in most instances he is a simple man. As for the little fellow, he thrives on those things.

Many of us play a part, some of the time. We act one way at work and another at play. We may be kind and sweet at home but harsh and unyielding to those under us at work; we may be the life of the party at a social gathering and a surly, grumpy person at home; an overgenerous host when strangers are around but a penny-pincher in the bosom of our immediate family.

Of course, a certain amount of play-acting is often required-call it polish, propriety or company manners. We would like to tell the truth, to reveal our true feelings but we cannot do it for the moment and must be polite and friendly and solicitous. The danger lies in carrying pretense too far, in wearing the false front too long, in making believe too often. Then it becomes a form of escape and leads to trouble.

Dramatizing yourself too much, exaggerating every trivial incident, ascribing undue importance to petty things and overacting on the slightest provocation is nerve-wracking. Pretending that you are somebody else and making a poor job of it is to undermine self-confidence, lose your own identity and become a "nobody". Pretense and dramatics may gain you temporary sympathy or attention but they seldom last and usually leave a bad taste with all concerned.

Guard your health and be your natural self. Capitalize upon what you have and what you are. Be simple, friendly, pleasant. All of this will lighten your load, brighten your day and add to the joys, the beauty and the richness of your life.

The Fourth Hour

ARE YOU SET IN YOUR WAYS?

You MAY DENY IT even to yourself but your views, ideas, sentiments, beliefs, opinions and conclusions are influenced by what you were and what you are.

In a sense, you are the product of your background, your experiences and your environment. Some of it has been forced upon you and the rest is of your own making.

This influence began in your infancy and has been at work ever since. It formed your likes and dislikes, molded your thoughts, engendered your beliefs, fostered your conclusions, affected your actions and conditioned your responses.

It began with your parents and the members of your family, with your father's occupation and his love or hatred for it, with his contacts and affiliations at work and elsewhere, with his character and educational background, with your home surroundings and your mother's homemaking, with your family's status in the neighborhood and the community, with your parents' social and religious contacts, with what was said or discussed in your presence and with what you were encouraged to do or not to do. All of these had a tremendous influence in shaping your character, in forming your concepts and in establishing your mode of general behavior.

Later came your school years, your teachers and classmates, the friends you made, the work or profession you chose, the interests you developed, the mate you selected, the family you raised, the standing you maintained. You were affected by the successes and failures you had, the disappointments you met, the grievances you nurtured, the social contacts you cultivated and the leisure time activities you followed. These became the background and the pattern for your habitual reactions and in turn conditioned your beliefs and convictions.

This is true of you and of all of us. As a result of such beliefs, feelings and convictions, many of us are opinionated and even prejudiced. Our minds are closed to changes or to the slightest deviations from what we believe in and from what we approve. On the other hand, there are those among us who remain tolerant and open-minded, who leave room for a divergence in belief and opinion, who make allowances for and accept differences in views, in concepts, in behavior and in conclusions.

Where do you stand? To what group do you belong? Test yourself. The following two sets of questions honestly answered, although not inclusive, will tell you many things about yourself. Their sequence is not an indication of their value or importance. They are intended for your private, personal use. Do not glide over them or give pat answers. Be as honest and as conscientious as you can. Put your answers down on paper and do not justify them.

1. How good are you at thinking things through? Can you weigh all angles, evaluate all possibilities and arrive at an impar-

tial decision? How sure are you of yourself when you reach such a decision? How quick are you to change it when others do not like it or criticize you? How far will you go to try to convince others that you are right and they should follow you?

2. How good are you at noticing things? How easy is it to dis turb you, to distract or to confuse you? How quick are you to sense dissension or disapproval? Can you evaluate someone else's idea or suggestion, in its proper light, without the personal angle?

3. How good are you at recalling names, faces, numbers, dates or details? How well do you remember facts and figures relating to something of interest to you? How accurate are you in making estimates or in arriving at conclusions? Do you base such on all the related factors or let your feelings, your hunches, beliefs or surmises sway you?

4. How good is your imagination? Is it of a practical nature? Can you direct it into constructive channels? Can you visualize newer, better and more effective ways of doing things? Can you describe them plainly, vividly, concretely to others so that they could see them through your eyes and lend you needed support and encouragement?

5. How good are you in your reasoning ability? Can you give sound, valid, specific reasons why you think or feel or act as you do? Do you take time out to explain to others, especially those under you, why you did or intend to do certain things if explana tions are in place and are expected of you? Do you usually stop to consider the rights, the privileges and the sensibilities of others, when they are working with you or for you, or do you think only of your own benefits and interests?

6. How quick are you to admit when you are wrong about something? Do you ever accept the blame so as to shield or pro tect others, weaker than you, in situations where you can do so, without harm to yourself? How do you react to justified or un justified opposition to your plans, wishes or desires? Do you ever feel that opposition is often desirable and even beneficial? How big a price would you pay to have your way?

7. Do you consider yourself a leader or a follower? Do you pre fer to follow the old beaten path or would you rather blaze a new

trail, even if the going is rough and uncertain? Do you have confidence in your ability to go at things alone, if you have to, or must
you have the support of others to go ahead?

8. How susceptible are you to suggestion? Do you readily ac
cept someone else's opinion or do you weigh it first in the light
of your own knowledge and experience? Are you awed by or are
you subservient to those with names, titles, position or badges of
office? Do you consider yourself the equal of, or above those with
whom you usually associate?

9. Are you usually cheerful and easy-going? Do changes in the
weather tend to affect you emotionally? How do you react to oc
casional set-backs or disappointments? Do you have a tendency to
fume, to fret and to complain about things you cannot change?
When you join others in any activity do you add something to it
or do you dampen the prevailing spirit? What tends to please you
most? What makes you feel sad, blue or dejected?

10. How good are you at your word? Are you rash in making
promises or do you keep every promise made? Can you be relied
upon to carry through whatever task undertaken, without being
prodded, reminded, checked or supervised? How loyal are you to
a cause, to a friend, to a course of action?

11. How cooperative are you when working with others on a
common project? Are you amenable, adaptable and dependable as
a member of a team or do you prefer to work as a lone wolf? Do
you insist that things be handled your way or else refuse to "play"?

12. How much enthusiasm can you generate to keep yourself
and others going when things are tough? Can you delegate re
sponsibility and choose the right person for the job or do you feel
that only you can do it right? How much does it take to discourage
you and "stop you cold"?

13. How do you act when you are suddenly placed in charge of
a certain job or project? Do you assume new airs or work amiably
with others as before? Do you begin to throw your weight around
or really lend a hand to do the job right? How much does it take
to make you feel all-important?

14. What are your pet peeves? How much does it take to have
you carry a grudge and nurture a grievance? What particular traits,

habits, mannerisms or characteristics in others irk you the most?

The additional twenty-five questions following touch upon other possible reactions and when honestly answered will tell you more about yourself. Be sure to give the reasons *why* you feel or react as you do. 1. Do you deal with or readily associate with those who are not of your faith? 2. What is your general attitude towards Negroes, Jews, Orientals, Christians, Moslems, Hindus and so-called foreigners, who live in or conduct businesses in your community? 3. Do you differentiate between them or do you class them as nondesirables? 4. What is your interpretation of an immoral, indecent, improper or sinful act? 5. Are they all evil and sinful in your eyes or do you allow for demarcations?

6. What is your definition of success, in its literal and connotative meaning? 7. How do you feel about monopolies and big business versus little business and the small man? 8. As you see it, can communism or any other ism live side by side with our way of life? 9. What type of plays and stories do you like best and why? 10. Do you hate anyone or anything with or without any reason? 11. What do you do for diversion? 12. How do you feel about armament races and the ever-mounting stockpiles of war materiel? 13. Do you favor an open shop policy or strongly organized labor and why? 14. What is your most memorable and enjoyable personal experience? 15. If you could start all over again what line of work would you choose and why?

16. How do you feel about government subsidies and private exploitation of our natural resources? 17. What are your pet aversions? 18. How would you handle the narcotics problem? 19. How would you deal with juvenile delinquents? 20. If you had the power what laws would you kill and what others would you put into immediate effect?

21. What are, in your opinion, the most desirable traits in a man? 22. Would you consider the same traits just as desirable in a woman? 23. What are the things you believe in? 24. If you could have two wishes realized what would you wish for? 25. What would make you the happiest person alive?

Consider each question separately and give it thought. The

answers are for your eyes only and unless you are honest with yourself the basic purpose of this self-analysis will be lost. So—be frank, outspoken, and write your answers in full.

The questions asked may appear to be running far afield but there is a purpose behind them. They are intended to help you take stock of how you feel about certain things and how you react to given conditions and situations.

Pause at every question and let your answer be a true inventory of your feeling about the matter so that at the end you will know what your views, sentiments, beliefs, opinions and convictions are.

Do not gloss over the questions and be satisfied with a simple "Yes" or "No", or with a cursory flippant remark, and should a given question evoke a lengthy reply do not cut it short.

Take all the time you need to give a frank answer to every question and having finished put your notes away somewhere and let them "age" for a while. Then when you look through them again a few days later try to see them with the eyes of a stranger, as if they were the intimate revelations of a dear friend.

Assume for the moment that this friend of yours is asking for your help to improve himself and in the light of such assumption tell him why some of his beliefs or convictions need to be changed or dropped entirely. Then, and only then, will you be taking another step to better, brighter days as you continue climbing upward on your stairway to success and happiness, only twenty-six space hours away.

The Fifth Hour

HOW TO CHANGE YOUR HABITS

WHEN A GIVEN ACTION is repeated so many times that it turns into a fixed tendency or an inclination and becomes almost automatic in its repetitive response it is called a habit.

Some habits are a conscious and deliberate attempt to establish the automatic response, others come by accident or unintentionally. For instance, if you were to assume a slouch because of pain in a shoulder and continued slouching until it became an habitual posture that would be a habit formed by accident. But, if you were to train your hands to press certain typewriter keys over and over again without watching the placement of your fingers and thus learned to do touch-typing unhesitatingly, you would be utilizing the power of habit to do what you want to do, knowingly, deliberately, automatically.

Habits are an important part of life for without them living would be a constant strain upon your nervous system and make life almost unbearable.

The right habit is a boon, a friend, a saver of effort and energy, a true blessing. The bad habit is a vice, a scourge, a despotical master. Habits can be your loyal slaves or your implacable enemies, because they affect your thoughts, influence your feelings, control your actions and replace natural urges and responses. They do it so simply, naturally, effortlessly, that nothing habitual ever seems to be odd or appears to be out of the ordinary. A story is told of a conniving merchant who grew so used to cheating others that in totaling his day's receipts and depositing them in the cashbox he began to short-change and cheat on himself.

Habits are easy to form but once set and established are almost impossible to break. The only way in which the power of an entrenched habit can be minimized or effectively blocked is by the gradual introduction of disturbing and conflicting changes in the time element, in the mode of operation and in the habitual procedure.

Let us assume that you are a chain smoker and for reasons of health must break that habit. You may have a strong will power and stop smoking because you will it so. But in most cases the craving will remain and the imbedded tendency will be too strong to be completely ignored or discarded. Somewhere along the line you will be tempted to take one surreptitious smoke and then another and soon the old habit will reassert itself.

The only way in which you can crack the solid, impenetrable

walls of the habit successfully is to attack it gradually, consistently, on one or more of these fronts:

1st. The "time-delay" attack.

Introduce a time change in the usual smoking routine. Start with a five minute interval between smokes. Make it five minutes to the second. As soon as the time is up pat yourself mentally on the back for having the strength of character shown, light your cigarette and enjoy every puff of it. Keep up this five minute interval between smokes, consistently, until it stops being a hardship and becomes the new habit, of lighting cigarettes five minutes apart.

Lengthen the interval between smokes to ten minutes and then to fifteen minutes each. Turn the waiting period into a little game or a contest. If you have nothing else to do to occupy the time in between, improvise some form of temporary diversion to while away the passing moments. Continue this waiting period in a playful mood until the new interval between smokes becomes part of your regular smoking habit.

2nd. The "time-check" attack.

Use your clock or your watch as a monitor, as a control to confine your smoking to certain periods. Let it be exactly on the half-hour and the full hour during the day, and the quarter hour and three-quarter hour during the evening. The underlying purpose is not to turn you into a clock-watcher but to give you a measuring or limiting control to help you inject an arbitrary time element into the customary smoking schedule and thereby interfere with your entrenched smoking habit.

yd. The "time-out" attack.

Set aside certain periods of time during your waking hours when you will refuse to light a cigarette no matter how strong the urge. Let it be a "break" a "stay-away" time when you use your will power, when you place yourself under absolute control for the ensuing period of time. The period selected and the duration of such self-restraint is not as important as the deliberate premeditated step you have taken to oppose the call of the habit and purposely interfere with its entrenched routine.

4th. *The "interference" attack.*

Change the usual mode and manner of smoking by introducing different disturbing elements. For instance, if you enjoy smoking best by sitting down or leaning back in your seat, get up and remain standing or start walking around the room while puffing away at your cigarette. If you are in the habit of taking long, leisurely puffs, change to short, nervous pulls at the cigarette. If you usually inhale stop doing it. If you wait ordinarily between puffs and let the smoke out lazily, bunch the puffs together. In other words, mix things up and keep changing your way of smoking from one cigarette to the next. Do it consistently, deliberately, consciously. Introduce as much confusion as you can contrive so that the old smooth continuity of the smoking habit will be disrupted.

5th. *The "substitution[7] attack.*

Change brands of cigarettes, from a regular to a King size, to a filter type, to one having mint or menthol in it, to a brand milder or stronger. If that does not help much change to a pipe or to stogies. Then, in between, pop a piece of hard candy or a stick of chewing gum into your mouth instead of a smoke. Give your lips and your mouth something else to do for the time being. Continue such substitutions until your system begins to accept them as part of, or in lieu of, the old smoking habit and eventually its hold upon you will be weakened and nullified.

These five ways of gradual frontal attack and deliberate interruptions with your set pattern of the smoking habit can be adapted to attack and interfere with any other non-desirable habit and prove just as effective in breaking its hold upon you.

New habits are easy to form and to give such formation the desired push use one or more of these suggestions:

1. Know exactly what the habit is supposed to do for you and give it the necessary room to get started properly.

2. Begin the new habit with a voiced pledge or with a written resolution. Refer to it often and use it as a constant guide, re minder or generator to keep building the new habit.

3. If the habit is dependent upon certain "if s", "when's" or specific circumstances, wait until they are in line before going ahead with the new habit.

4. Set up for yourself a definite plan or mode of operation and hold the time, the place, the method or the manner of such pro cedure inviolable.

5. Do not allow yourself to deviate in the slightest from the original procedure unless such deviation is to become part of your new habit.

6. Be consistent. Keep repeating the same procedure in the same way at the same time and in the same manner, time after time, until the tendency to repeat asserts itself and the newly-formed habit takes over.

In addition to their values as servants, friends and supporters habits have another important function. They are part of your natural defense system. They act as shock-absorbers to cushion the blows and the impacts of life upon you.

The complexities of modern living, even under the most ideal conditions, make it almost impossible for you to realize all your dreams for ease and comfort, for financial security, for satisfaction or for happiness. Somewhere along the line, sooner or later, you will meet sorrow, defeat, trouble, sickness, worry, anxiety, handicaps, disappointments and even tragedy. Somewhere along the way you may be stopped in your tracks and be forced to readjust yourself to new conditions or make a complete "about face" in all of your original plans, hopes, wishes and desires.

To do this properly you have to learn how to protect yourself, as much as possible, from those sudden blows and unexpected impacts of life. You have to learn how to go over the rough spots as smoothly as you can with the least wear and tear on your physical and nervous system.

Fortunately for you, nature has endowed you with two lines of defense. They are supplemented by tremendous reserves which you can muster into service at a moment's notice.

Your first line of defense is your senses. You are the center of your own little world. As William Henley put it so beautifully in his immortal poem "Invictus", ". . . You are the master of your fate, you are the captain of your soul". Nothing can reach you, figuratively speaking, unless it comes through your senses. They color it, filter it, modify it, amplify it, intensify or nullify it, and thus things can touch you or affect you only to such extent as you allow.

Your second line of defense is your feelings and emotions. There, too, you exercise the prerogative of being the master of your fate and the captain of your soul. You can control your feelings and emotions. Yon can hold them in check, as it were, and thus offset or counteract, increase or decrease, accept or reject the impact of conditions and circumstances upon you.

Your reserves are in the invincible, unshakable power of the habits you formed. They can take precedence over your first and second lines of defense and preclude possible harm to you. They can be veritable phalanxes of power to shield you and protect you from direct onslaught, in numerous ways.

For instance, if you formed the habit of being cheerful, easy-going, even tempered or good-natured it would be almost impossible for anyone to pick a fight or an argument with you and upset your serenity. Likewise, if you formed the habit of looking for good in others and staying on the sunny side of the street you will normally overlook the frailties of man, the annoyances of the day, and will not be affected so much by the gloomy, seamy side of life.

On the other hand, if you are in the habit of finding fault with people and things or conditions about you, you will have many reasons for being unhappy and your troubles will be increased a hundredfold. Furthermore, if you formed the habit to carry a chip on your shoulder somebody is sure to knock it off someday and perhaps knock you down at the same time.

Make your habits work for you. Discard the harmful ones and replace them with those that will be your loyal friends, your best supporters, your reserves of strength and stamina. You can do it. It may take a little time and effort on your part, but it will be worth it. And while you are about it surround those new habits with imagination, with clear thinking and with self-confidence. Let them strengthen your private little world and add joy and beauty to it.

By imagination is meant clear-cut visualization of what you want to do and what you want to be. It is setting a specific goal for yourself, with something to work for and to strive for. It is mapping a course of action and application and checking yourself from time to time to be sure you are on the right course. Without such directive visualization you will be drifting aimlessly along and can hardly ever expect to reach a set destination. It is not too late to get started now and the mere fact that you came this far, speaks well for you.

So—put your directive imagination to work. Plan your future and work at it. Fill your mind with positive, cheerful, constructive thoughts. Know where you are going and while you are on your way plan to improve your personality, to capitalize upon your abilities and to get more out of every day's living.

By clear thinking is meant sensible, practical support of your imaginative faculties but be sure to differentiate between day dreaming and constructive, purposeful thought. Study and evaluate your potentialities and follow through on the interests and the inclinations which best express your basic personality. That is where you can do the most for yourself.

By self-confidence is meant self-assurance, self-reliance, self-esteem and self-control, all important adjuncts and attributes of a winning personality. This indicates the ability to judge and evaluate the good and the bad of everything that might face you and arriving at the right decision. It stands for the readiness to face opposition, whether or not it is justifiable, without flinching or resentment. It signifies the willingness to take on obligations and shoulder responsibilities. It stands for the courage to identify yourself fully, wholeheartedly, with whatever task you have undertaken and the tenacity to carry it through to a successful conclusion.

It also implies having control over your feelings and emotions and never letting bad temper master you, to the detriment of all concerned. It further implies having the proper regard for your own values and never, under any pretext or provocation, selling yourself short.

Keep your lines of defense ever ready to protect you. Supplement them with the tremendous reserves of the right habits backed by constructive thought, directive imagination and properly applied self-confidence. Then as surely as you breathe and live you will be the master of your fate and the captain of your soul.

The Sixth Hour

MAKE MEMORY WORK FOR YOU

MANY OF US start a collection of one sort or another early in life and as the years go by either drop it entirely or continue it, in some other form.

The youngster may start with stamps or coins, with match boxes or butterflies, with cowboy pictures or sport heroes. As he grows older he often follows new interests and starts to collect records or pennants, programs or photographs of favorite movie stars. The business or professional man turns to antiques, to early Americana, to first editions or to objects of art.

The urge to collect is the natural expression of the desire to own things and when kept up moderately, sensibly, has many points in its favor. It provides a desirable diversion, brings a measure of relaxation, regenerates flagging spirits, engenders a sense of personal importance, satisfies the urge to have something to show off with or to talk about, adds to one's self-esteem and often makes the collector feel that he is contributing something tangible to man's store of lore and knowledge. It also supplies him with special thrills and a sense of elation when he can complete a set or add something especially rare and valuable to his collection.

Many of the prized possessions of museums, of inestimable value to students and researchers, were started originally as private collections and were later willed or donated to the public institutions.

You may have never been a collector and perhaps cannot boast of having added anything to the collections of art, of industry, of man's march through the ages or of unusual odds and ends. Yet, strange as it sounds, you have with you at all times one of the best and greatest collections ever gathered by man. It is as large and varied and colorful as life itself. It is part of you and as such is closely identified with everything that you are, were or will be.

The collection grows day by day, yet it requires no attention on your part, involves no work or expenditures and calls for no special facilities or aptitudes to collect, to classify and to maintain itself in tip-top condition. Yet, you can display it at will, share it readily with others as often as you like and still retain it in its entirety as your very own.

It is just another of the amazing wonders with which nature has endowed you and which you can utilize at will. It is the marvel of all depositories—your memory. And with what ease it can bring back to you all the pleasant memories of the past! How quickly it can span time and space and recall for you, in their minutest detail, moments of joy, of bliss, of exultation!

Your ability to store impressions is unlimited and your memory's capacity to recall them is practically inexhaustible. We do not know exactly how memory works. Some psychologists believe that memory is an impression upon a sensitized cell which becomes one of the links in an interlocked chain of similarly impressed cells. Others feel that memory is an electro-chemical deposit charged or etched into a loop of cells by tiny tendrils which remain forever saturated with the original charge.

Whatever be the way memory works it has billions of separate sensitive brain cells at its disposal. Each cell is a recorder and a transmitter, a lead and a follow-up, a prompter and controller. Each cell is capable of accepting, retaining, combining and coordinating its own impression with others in a bewildering fashion.

There, among the countless nerve cells comprising your memory files, everything you have ever seen, heard, touched, felt, tasted, known or experienced is duly recorded and can be recalled, with or without your volition, in fractions of a second.

Some of those impressions leave the level of conscious recall and appear to be lost but they are never forgotten. They become imbedded in the vast labyrinths of your unconscious mind. There many of them remain dormant through life but others start to combine into groups, one mounting atop another, until they gather size and strength and reach the explosive point. The explosion may be a harmless one and spend itself in some simple devious way or it may turn into a complex, a fixation or a neurosis.

No one ever uses the full power of his memory. Psychologists contend that the average person uses less than ten percent of his memory's capacity to retain and to remember. But we differ in our abilities to memorize. Some do it best by utilizing the visual sense, others by using the auditory or the motor senses. Find out which is the easier way for you to memorize and put it to use.

For instance, if you find that you memorize best by ear, be sure to read aloud the things you want to remember. Do it several times and listen particularly to the sounds of the words as you enunciate them. If your *forte* are sight impressions try to look at everything you wish to remember as if your eyes were a camera lens and you were focusing them time and again upon a given object to be photographed. And, if you memorize best by movement try to associate motion and action with the things you wish to remember. Or, use a combination of these ways so that you will find it much easier to recall things and make memory work for you.

Let memory help you utilize nature's golden treasures, for tomorrow morning and every morning thereafter she will hand you one of her most precious gifts, twenty-four new, fresh, virgin hours of time. They will be yours without provisions or restrictions, yours to use as you wish and the way you utilize them will determine how much good, joy, pleasure and satisfaction they will bring you.

Of course, some of those hours will be taken up with work, food, sleep, play and the other ordinary pursuits of the day. But what about the rest of the time? What about the free hours or fractions of them when you are not doing anything, when you are throwing time away unthinkingly, when you could devote such time to something useful, desirable and enjoyable?

You might ask what you could do during those spare moments scattered through the day and the answer is, do what you have been wanting to do. You can widen your horizons, improve your mind, make new contacts, form new friendships, learn something new and different and make over your entire world.

There must be things you wanted to do, studies you planned to take up, people you wanted to meet, places you wanted to visit, sights you wanted to see, hobbies you wanted to follow, dreams or ambitions you hoped to fulfill. Then go about them now.

Perhaps you have been waiting for that far-off day when you will have full hours, days or weeks at your disposal and thus be able to follow your particular bent or inclination. But, keep in mind this salient fact: only ten or twenty minutes a day multiplied by weeks or months pile up fast and give you all the time needed —right now.

You will never have all the spare time you want to do this or that. There will always be something to hold you back, work or sickness, company or family, poor weather or the wrong mood, or something more desirable to do for the moment. Yet, strangely enough, once you start that long-delayed activity and become interested in what you are doing or trying to do, you will find the time to go ahead, without difficulty.

Start now, in a small way, within the spare time you have. Your beginning need not involve drastic changes in your usual daily routine or take time away from what you must do, day by day. For instance, supposing you wanted to learn French and could devote only fifteen minutes a day to it. That time is enough to enable you to learn three or four new words. Within a year you would know upwards of a thousand French words, more than enough to be able to read, to speak and to understand the ordinary French conversation.

Here is how one man took up learning French. He was always fond of the story of the "Count of Monte Cristo" and decided to read it in the original. His local librarian supplied him with the copies of the novel in French and a literal translation in English. He read the original with the aid of the translation and a dictionary. He tackled next "The Three Musketeers" in the same way and by the time he finished the two novels, translating the French into English line by line, and literally word by word, he knew enough French to be able to join a local French group and adequately understand a French newspaper. He visited Canada several times and listening to him speak French you would swear he was a born Frenchman.

Nearly twenty-seven hundred years ago the Chinese philosopher Lao-tse said that no one has to leave his own armchair to see the world. So—if you have been wanting to visit the Orient, for instance, and cannot take the trip now, do it via the armchair route. Your librarian can easily supply you with maps, books, travelogues and vivid accounts of trips to different parts of the Orient. This can provide you with many opportunities to learn the customs, habits, traditions, folk-lore and national characteristics of every nation in the Orient. It can familiarize you with every point of interest, with the facts and details of everything worth knowing. In fact, it can make you an authority on the Orient.

Then when you can finally take the trip you would be deriving more pleasure from it than any other fellow traveler. You would know what to look for and where to find it. You would know what to do when you get there and how to appreciate the things you see. You would be able to speak intelligently, interestingly, authoritatively about the people, their customs and traditions. Thus, in a sense, you would be the guide, the leader, the pacesetter for all of the other members of the same touring party, someone who would stand out head and shoulders above the rest.

You have a priceless collection in the vaults of your memory. You have another golden gift in the brand-new twenty-four hours which nature places at your disposal every morning. Let the spare moments you have help you fill your storehouse of memory with joyful and pleasant impressions. Let them brighten each day as time passes by and let them add to the joys and contentment of your life.

Make memory serve you well. Keep it well stocked and then you shall always have at your command a treasurehouse of inexhaustible comfort and pleasure. That is what Moore had in mind when he wrote:

> *When time who steals our years away*
> *Shall steal our pleasures too;*
> *The mem-ry of the past will stay*
> *And half our joys renew.*

The Seventh Hour

WHAT IS YOUR PSYCHIC AGE?

THIS IS THE SEVENTH DAY in your thirty-day, thirty-hour climb to better, brighter and happier days. If you retained the original premise that you are climbing a thirty-step stairway to success and happiness, you have gone up seven steps. You are now seven space hours away from your starting point and have reached your first landing.

From this landing you can look down, seven feet below you, and see what you have gained. You have reviewed some old, familiar things and learned a few new ones. You have a better concept of what and who you are, a fuller understanding of the many "you's" in you, and can appreciate the close relationship between physical and mental health. You have had the opportunity to check into your views and opinions, to know how habits are formulated and how to make memory work for you.

Now it is time to consider your psychic age, but first ask yourself what IS age? What is the right or the wrong number of years to admit as your own? How do you determine the relationship between calendar years and looks, feeling, interests and activities? Why should any shame or stigma be attached to the fact that you have seen a given number of calendar years? Of course, there may be times, due to real or fancied reasons, when you will find it expedient to take off a few years. But otherwise why lie about your age? Why attach so much importance to youth when it *is* the formative period in life?

Age is a projection of time as we interpret it and time is a relative term. It is both static and dynamic. It can be as fleeting as a sudden gust of wind and as interminable as desert heat in the middle of day.

Age is not a matter of birthdays. Biologically speaking, the older you grow the slower the aging process. You change more, physically and mentally, from age ten to twenty than from thirty to fifty and there is hardly any aging from 60 to 70.

Furthermore, not all the parts of your body age in the same degree. Your eyes begin to age at ten, your hearing at twenty, your muscular activity at thirty and the brain after sixty. On the basis of your birthdays you may be "XX" years old but judged by your mental, physical and spiritual responses you may be years younger. You are as old as you feel, think, act and respond. You can be old at forty and young at seventy.

Walter Pitkin in his best seller "Life Begins at Forty" emphasizes over and over again that youth is in the red, that life after forty is more exciting, interesting and exhilarating. According to his contentions, and he advances facts and figures to substantiate his claims, life *begins* at forty.

As he puts it: "Grubbing for a mere existence is no longer a dawn-to-dusk chore. Serfdom and feudalism were wiped out years ago. Decimating diseases have been eliminated. With increased popular education, with greater medical care and attention, with better health provisions and with improved standards of living men and women past forty are only beginning to live and to enjoy life. And they have all the advantages over youth. . . ."

Pitkin continues: "As a matter of record people can get more out of their fourth, fifth and sixth decades of life than out of any other earlier period in their life, simply by knowing how to live and how to make the most of every opportunity presented to them. . . ."

And Pitkin is right. If you are past forty you have already weathered many of life's storms. You have gone through the schooling and the preparation period. You learned a trade or a profession or started a business. You married, bought a home, raised a family and established yourself within your community. You made a place for yourself among your friends, co-workers or associates and life around you. You gained stature and have more knowledge, experience, contacts and background than ever before. And by the same token you have more opportunities to live and to enjoy life than any of the kings or monarch's of old, especially with the improvements and the discoveries of our modern age.

The secret of staying young at forty, fifty, sixty and over lies not in physical measurements, in looks or contours, in social or sport activities but in retaining an alert and active mind. Aging begins when we settle down to a sedentary animalistic existence, when we allow ourselves to vegetate, when we lose interest in everything else but food, sleep, comfort and the telling of the pains or operations we had.

No one can foretell how long he will live and neither can you. Yet it is safe to say that barring serious accidents, epidemics or disabling sicknesses, you will live as long as you guard your health, avoid excesses of any nature, and as long as you prepare yourself to live.

There are people who consider themselves ancients at sixty or thereabouts. They stop working or keeping themselves busy at something. They become preoccupied with their health and the hereafter. A minor ailment assumes major proportions with them and they intensify it by mounting fears, worries and lamentations. They prepare themselves mentally, spiritually and psychically to die and before long their expectations are materialized.

On the other hand, there are others, age sixty or over, who look at life sensibly and maintain a healthy mental attitude about their age. They do not abuse themselves or overtax their physical limitations but at the same time they do not pamper themselves or magnify their occasional discomforts. They take a sickness or a temporary disability in their stride, as a natural happening in older age, and try to get over it as lightly and normally as possible. They retain an interest in the people and the world around them and keep themselves mentally alert and youthful.

They refuse to accept their calendar years as evidence of disability or as a measure of their usefulness. They remain active and young in mind and in spirit, even when they have to slow down in their usual physical activities and have to be more mindful of the food they eat. They make allowances for changes, for new trends and innovations. They avoid being stubborn or dictatorial, and try to adapt themselves to the newer conditions. The evils of idle hands and idle minds or the debilitating effects of watching for the symptoms of old age cannot touch them or affect them. As a result, they live on and on, far beyond the accepted three score and ten, and evidence of such longevity is all around you.

To which group do you belong? If to the second, you are to be congratulated; if to the first, you still have time to mend your ways and benefit by them. Now is the time to do it, because never again shall you have the same opportunity to do something about adding more life to your years.

Victor Hugo said nearly one hundred years ago: "Forty is the old age of youth; fifty is the youth of old age. . . ." Take this thought to mind, use it as a guide to set your goals, and let it help you to orientate yourself.

To paraphrase Elbert Hubbard: "There are many misguided souls who wear themselves out too soon by trying to live in three different worlds at one time, the past, the present and the future . . . Why shorten your life? Why take on the added burdens of dragging the dreary past behind you? Why tack on the uncertainties of the future and put off living and enjoying the present?

"If you made mistakes in the past, your reparation lies not in regrets or self-recriminations but in the thankfulness that you know better now and will not repeat the same mistakes . . . If you were selfish, unkind, forgetful or inconsiderate in the past be thankful you are in the present and can do something to redeem your past. Consider the future and plan for it but do not let it weigh you down with assumptions or probabilities . . . Thank God for this day, in which you can work and live and perhaps do a little good . . ."

How right Hubbard was! It is a glorious feeling to be alive, to see, to hear, to listen, to taste, to feel and to be able to dream. It is a privilege to meet life, to love, to laugh, to make friends, to enjoy and to appreciate beauty all around us, from the blue sky up on high to the blossoming flower swaying gently in the breeze to the happy and carefree laughter of a child.

Nothing is inert and nothing goes to complete waste in nature. Nothing stands still and nothing dies completely. Forms, substances and molecular combinations change but life goes on and

on. Air, water and chemical compounds form animate and inanimate life. That, in turn, goes through a cycle of birth, growth,
maturity and death, returns into dust or seeming disintegration
but soon afterwards the same process starts all over again.

Forget your calendar years and find something to keep your
hands and your mind busy. There are no limits to what you can
undertake. Cultivate the company of younger people as well as
those nearer your age. Get yourself a pet. Join a music or an art
class. Take up dancing, singing, gardening, writing or whatever
appeals to you, even if it be only for the fun of it.

Discard the old and sentimental things, so useless now, and
blossom out anew. Develop a new hobby or start teaching yours
to others. The big, wide, wonderful world of ours is spread out
before you in all its splendor and it offers you so much . . . Find
something there to keep you mentally and physically alert and
active and no matter how many calendar years are added to your
age you will never be old.

And while we are on the subject of age, have you reached your
menopause or climacteric period in life? Have you developed the
strange sickness of the middle-age let-down, the creeping fear that
you have come to the end of your usefulness and will now have
to step aside for others, younger than you?

This middle-age let-down becomes a growing dissatisfaction with
what you are, with what you have accomplished and with what
the future holds for you. It is a sense of inadequacy and futility.

In the case of a man with a job and responsibilities, who ful-
filled his duties as a worker, a husband, a father and provider for
his family, this middle-age sickness becomes a growing insidious
suspicion that all of his younger associates, co-workers or subor-
dinates are watching him constantly, hoping that he will slip or
have to slow down and thus have a legitimate excuse to push him
aside and step into his shoes. This frame of mind turns his suspicions into open antagonism and makes him short-tempered. He
becomes hard to work with, tends to add fear to his assumed burdens and intensifies his feeling of a let-down.

In the case of a man in the professions or in the business world
the middle-age sickness becomes a conviction that he is losing

ground, that his competitors are stealing his customers or his clientele. He plunges deeper into work, expands to the danger point, takes wild chances and begins to drive himself mercilessly. This begins to tell after a while and he succeeds in making a physical and nervous wreck of himself.

In the case of a man who is semi-retired and is no longer burdened with business, family or financial worries, the climacteric age often brings his marital or sexual life to the fore. He starts to compare his wife to other younger, and more attractive, women. He begins to wonder about his waning manhood, develops a roving eye and enters into questionable romantic interludes and entanglements, with ensuing disastrous results.

Middle age and the coming of the menopause often takes many a woman by surprise. The emotional disturbances often start long before the irregularities in her menstrual periods begin and she is hardly prepared for them. Hence, her heat waves, backaches and despondency moods are usually aggravated by fear, worry and anxiety.

Some women accept that transition period with grace, dignity, forbearance and equanimity. Others fight it all the way. They become irritable, depressed, easily upset, capricious, hard to live with, or they begin to pay excessive attention to their looks, their contours and their clothes.

Many women begin to brood about love passing them by, about their seemingly waning feminine appeal. They crave attention and in their anxiety to find romance seek it in the most unlikely places. They become easy prey for con-men and adventurers and in its wake bring troubles and heartbreak upon themselves.

All of these men and women fail to remember that the climacteric age and the menopause are transition periods in their respective lives. It is one of the peaks in their journey through the years and properly evaluated will surely lead them to other crests along the way.

Many older people worship youth too much and bemoan the passing of years. They completely ignore the fact that youth is the stepping stone to life and not its ultimate end, and that there is no youth alive who does not hope and dreams and wants to grow older. So—if you reached middle age, managed to retain your health and attained a measure of success be glad. Do not bewail the coming years and do not fear the transition period. Love, marital intimacies and the zest for living life to the full will not be lost to you.

Take time to look around you. Note the hundreds of men and women considerably older than you who went through the same transition period and are now, seemingly, enjoying life. They, too, had the same fears, flushes, pains and despondent moments. They, too, felt insecure and inadequate, but the bad discouraging days passed and they are back in the swing of things and, in some instances, are doing better and are happier than before.

If you are still in the throes of your menopause or the climacteric age here are several ways to relieve your worries and minimize your anxieties.

1st. Stop being engrossed in your heat waves and discomforts. Accept them as they come and if they are too disconcerting ask your doctor for the proper medications.

2nd. Follow your usual routine at home, at work or at play but start to slow down a little, here and there.

3rd. Begin to transfer some of your interests and activities to your associates, co-workers, children or grandchildren and find pleasure in their advancements and accomplishments.

4th. Funnel some of your energies and activities into social, civic, fraternal or charitable sources and through sublimation derive new joys and satisfaction.

5th. Evaluate your position at work or in business. Consider your eventual retirement from actual arduous duties and start delegating responsibilities to others.

6th. Counteract your tension by taking up new diversions, by following your special bent or by acquiring a new hobby. These will provide new outlets for you and help to keep you young and active in interests outside of your usual routine.

7th. Accept the passage of the time and the natural physiological changes of your age in your stride and grow older gracefully.

Let youth look toward the distant future and work hard for it. Let youth hurry and strive for the older years to come. Your future is already here and you need no longer prepare yourself for it. Matured age has its joys, its pleasures, its thrills and compensations. Look for them, work at them, and your years to come will rest lightly and easily on your shoulders as you continue to climb steadily onward on your stairway to success and happiness, only twenty-three space hours away.

The Eighth Hour

WHAT PRICE TEMPER AND GRUDGES?

THE LOSS OF TEMPER and the carrying of a grudge have these things in common. Both foster emotional disturbances, both seek vindication and retaliation and both exact a terrific toll in the loss of amity, confidence, friendship and peace of mind.

How many times did you lose your temper recently? How many times did something, seemingly unimportant, set your teeth on edge and made you lose yourself in an outburst of rage?

Whether it happened only once or many times recently take time out now to look into the last one. Retrace your steps and do not start justifying yourself or finding excuses. Remember that your losses of temper are due to something that happens and what you are after, at the moment, is to know the underlying reasons.

So—start asking these questions of yourself and be truthful in your answers. When did you lose your temper last? How? Why? Who was involved? What brought it about? Could it have been prevented in any way? Did it accomplish anything? Could the same conditions or circumstances bring on another outburst? Would you want it to happen again? Who gained by it? Who lost by it? What was the final cost in loss of contacts or friendship?

Loss of temper is an indication of weakness, of the inability to contain one's self. It is the childish tantrums of the adult intended to be used in the same way, either to gain concessions or to block interference with one's whims and desires.

Loss of temper is often a mask for the sense of inadequacy, for the feeling of inferiority. The shouts or screams, the anger and the aroused indignation are used as a tool, a club or a crutch, to gain one's ends and have one's way.

Unfortunately, once loosened, temper cannot be held back. It becomes a temporary mental derangement and sweeps everything aside. It rides roughly over reason, honor, duty, loyalty, decency and common sense. In its inexorable sweep of passion it ignores the original purposes and tears everything apart.

To paraphrase Arnold Bennett: "A man who loses his temper starts a raging fire within himself and in all things around him that can never be put out . . . It is one of life's most shameful displays of abominable behavior . . . Dignity, justice, fairness, common sense and all that is close and dear is trampled mercilessly underfoot and destroyed. Wild passion stamps on the face of reason . . . The loss is great but the resultant shame and humiliation are often even greater . . ."

There are other losses, directly attributable to the loss of temper, which you might often overlook.

1. There is the impact upon your nervous system, the strong effect upon your endocrine glands, the excess acids and adrenalin poured into your blood stream, the strain on the heart, the over working of the liver, the disruption of normal digestive processes and bodily functions.

2. There is the emotional disturbance created, the uncontrol lable urge to strike back, to retaliate no matter what the cost, to hit, to hurt, to shame or to destroy.

3. There is the ensuing sense of shame or guilt, of sorrow or regret, of self-accusation or self-condemnation after the surge of the temper subsided when you have had the time to examine the ruins you left behind.

4. There is the anger, the resentment or the animosity you built up in others when you let go of your senses and did every thing you could to defy, degrade, shame, insult, belittle and hurt them.

5. Finally, there is the break between you and those involved, a break which can hardly ever be mended, a break which means that you have burned your bridges behind you and can never come back.

Strangely enough, the loss of temper is a habit formed gradually. It starts innocently with a raised voice or with simulated anger to gain a point. The other person gives in readily and a pattern of behavior has its beginning. The intensity of the shouts and the anger is gradually, deliberately increased, as more opposition is encountered and soon the loss of temper is firmly entrenched as a damaging habit and indisputable master.

If you are beset by that habit and wish to be rid of it, begin to chop at it steadily, consistently, in these ways: 1. Know what is at the root of your outburst and give it no chance to get started. 2. Put yourself on probation and dissipate as soon as you can every provocation of anger. 3. Ask friends or others to hoist the danger signal for you, when you fail to notice the tell-tale signs yourself. 4. Visualize loss of temper as a sign of weakness, as an indication of immaturity, as the mark of irresponsibility, as the humiliating spectacle of a fool. 5. Look for extenuating circumstances whenever you want to accuse, to condemn or to speak your mind freely.

One sure way to resist the urge to explode in the grip of temper is to clamp your lips tight, to sit down and lean back in your seat, to anchor your hands in your pockets and your feet to the floor and let the wave of temper pass over you. Then no matter how strong the temptation temper will not master you. Of course, the wish to assert yourself may be strong, but a display of bad temper is not desirable at any time.

Carrying a grudge is another form of nurturing a so-called wrong or injustice. It leads to anger, to resentment and to the urge of retaliation. It allows a petty misunderstanding to become a festering sore and a trivial annoyance to turn into a deep resentment. These often build up to an explosive display of temper.

A grudge is supposed to satisfy a spite, to give a temporary feeling of satisfaction and soothe wounded pride, but it exacts a tremendous price in the loss of good will, in regrets, in estrangements, in broken friendly relations and in emotional tension and no grudge is ever worth it.

Of course, there are times when you lose patience, when you must show anger or indignation, when in the height of such surge of emotion you do or say regrettable things. Such flare-ups are expected and are allowable under the circumstances. But what happens afterwards? What steps do you take later to mend broken fences, settle differences, adjust misunderstandings and resume friendly, amiable relations?

One simple, easy way to bridge the sudden gap and to resume normal relations is to be big enough to apologize, to admit the error of your ways if you happen to be in the wrong or feel that you are partly to blame, and try to patch things up as soon as possible. It is only the "small" in mental stature who hold on to foolish pride, who are afraid to "lose face", who would rather lose all than admit they could be wrong.

It is easy to take issues, to turn a slight into an offense. It is easy to act "biggety", to assume a belligerent attitude, to argue and to disagree at the mention of a word. It builds up one's ego but it also fosters resentments, engenders hatreds, magnifies minor discrepancies, upsets normal contacts and estranges friends.

It is surprising how quickly someone else's anger subsides when you step back and say you are sorry! How can he remain angry with you when you accept the blame and throw yourself upon his mercy and fair-mindedness? How can he continue to berate you when you stop opposing him and thus give him the opportunity to act big, important and forgiving?

This does not imply that you should turn into a doormat and let everybody walk over you, but rather that you do not evoke anger and disagreement unnecessarily, that you do not insist upon having your way all of the time, that you step back a pace or two when it is expedient.

This is true especially when you are part of a group and want to work harmoniously together toward a common goal, because even if you are in charge you can still allow for individual initiative and let someone else have the temporary limelight.

Even when you know you are right and yours is the only sensible, practical way of going about certain things, do not assume a "high-and-mighty" attitude and do not press your advantage too strongly. Ask for advice. Welcome discussion and opposition. Make believe you are not sure of your ground. Seek corroboration of your views and let others think that they hit upon the right solution. In other words, make people feel they are important to you, that you value their opinions, that you appreciate their efforts, and they will never get angry with you or nurture grudges against you.

You are more likely to get angry, to carry a grudge or to nurture a grievance when you feel sad and are in a dejected or discouraged mood. By the same token, you will perk up quicker, be less likely to take offense or become incensed when you are in a happy, high-spirited frame of mind.

These low and happy moods are said to be of a physiological nature. As endocrinologists explain it, we have our emotional "ups" and "downs" at regular intervals and in well-defined cycles. The secretions of our liver and the glands, and especially of the pituitary gland, set the rhythm for an emotional round-trip which completes its cycle from low to high and back again every thirty-three to thirty-six days.

At the height of the cycle, when there is an excess of energy, we feel great and sit on the top of the world. At the low point of the cycle when the surplus energy is exhausted we tire more easily, feel depressed more quickly, snap back at people more readily, grow fidgety, develop grudges and give in to moods of dejection.

Keep those emotional cycles in mind, when you have the blues and feel "mighty low". Keep them also in mind when others snap at you and find fault with you. It may be due to one of the phases in their emotional cycle and will soon pass.

Let no loss of temper or a grudge rule you. Retain control over your emotions and you will surely add to your happiness.

The Ninth Hour

PUT YOUR OWN ALADDIN LAMP TO WORK

THROUGH HUNDREDS OF YEARS readers and listeners alike have thrilled to the Arabian Nights' tale of Aladdin and his lamp. It is the personification of the wish-fulfillment to most of us but James Lowell gave it an entirely different interpretation as he wrote:

> *When I was a beggarly boy*
> *And lived in a cellar damp,*
> *I had neither friend nor toy*
> *But I had my Aladdin lamp.*
> *When I could not sleep for the cold*
> *I had fire enough in my brain;*
> *For I builded with roads of gold*
> *My beautiful Castles in Spain . . .*

Viewed in that concept you have an Aladdin lamp at your finger tips that can do wonders for you. It can take you far afield and bring you untold inner riches and contentment. It is in your heart, in your visions, in that inner imaginative quality which imbues our dreams, urges, impulses and desires with the invincible drive to give of ourselves wholly, full-heartedly, to whatever interests us, at the moment.

Children have it in abundance. You can see it in their faces and in their actions. You can hear it in their joyous outcries and carefree laughter as they pursue freely, with all the fullness of their hearts, whatever occupies them at the moment.

Those who dedicated themselves to a given cause or purpose also have it in abundance. You can tell it in their incessant drive against all set-backs and obstacles. You can see it in their repeated efforts to go on against all odds, not to gain fame, fortune or acclaim, but to complete their self-appointed tasks, and to satisfy that deep inner urge which cannot be stilled, ignored or denied.

We call it enthusiasm, and the dictionary defines it as intense interest, deep feeling, fervid zeal, ecstasy, eagerness, exaltation or fullness of heart.

"Nothing great was ever achieved without enthusiasm" said Emerson. His sentiments were echoed by Beaconsfield who said "Enthusiasm is the breath of genius", and by Lytton who said: "Nothing is so contagious as enthusiasm and truth accomplishes no victories without it".

Bishop Deans saw enthusiasm as the element of success in whatever might be undertaken, as the light that leads on, as the strength that lifts man in his efforts . . . While Brooks warned us not to lose our enthusiasm so that we could glory in something and ever retain our admiration for all that ennobles, enriches and beautifies our life.

And Henry Chester put it: "Enthusiasm is the greatest asset in the world. It beats money, power and influence . . . Single-handed the enthusiast can convince and dominate . . . Enthusiasm spurns inaction, tramples over prejudice and opposition, storms the citadel of its object, and like an avalanche overwhelms and engulfs all obstacles . . . It is nothing more or less than faith in action . . . Set the germ of enthusiasm afloat around you . . . Carry it in your attitude and manner . . . It means joy and pleasure . . . It means real, virile life . . ."

Never be afraid to become imbued with the fires of enthusiasm. It chases away gloom, doubt and despair. It is like the breath of spring in the midst of winter, like the glowing warmth of a bright sun on a frosty morning. It ignites ambition, spurs effort, intensifies desire, strengthens purpose, robs difficulty of its hardships and turns dreary, tedious toil into acts of joy and pleasure. No other motivating power can equal its driving force, its surge of stamina.

This builds quite a case for enthusiasm, but how do we go about acquiring it and cultivating it? The definitions give us a lead.

1. Intense interest. That is the first lead. It implies a strong

liking or preference, a deep desire, an imbedded urge. Nearly every one of us has a certain bent or inclination. It may be something we ignored through the years or followed only half-heartedly. It may be a forgotten urge recently brought to light or a newly acquired interest. Whatever the case, give it room to grow and express itself. Charge it with sustained interest, imbue it with deep feeling, sustain it with all of your will power, and you will have enthusiasm with you.

2. Fervid zeal. This is your second lead, the happy union of fervor and desire. It is like a gentle, constant flame that warms you but never burns or scorches. It is the innate or the acquired ability to give of yourself to a set task or cause, to a principle or belief, to some special urge or inclination, with body, mind and soul. It is a self-renewing, self-regenerating tenacity which cannot be broken, shaken or pushed aside. It is the invincible driving force that rekindles itself from its own failures again and again, and like the fabled Arabian bird, Phoenix, rises anew from its own ashes.

Your years will never weigh you down, your heart will never grow old and your questing spirit will ever be alert as long as you can foster intense interest and fervid zeal within you. But how to do it is something that you, and only you, can tell. It has to be something that touches the strings of your heart and makes them hum, sing, and vibrate with joy.

Of course, you may know exactly what it is that sets the strings of your heart a-singing and thus have no problem before you. On the other hand, you may not know which way to turn, because you have no special hobbies, aptitudes or inclinations.

If that be your case, turn the clock back and put your "bump of curiosity" to work for you once again. You had it years ago when as a child you used to bombard your parents, your teachers and your elders with all sorts of questions. Everything you saw, heard, touched, felt or could think of opened a new flood of questions. You kept asking "how?", "why?", "when?", "where?", "how come?", "what for?", and you could not be put off so easily. You kept at it until you were given a satisfactory answer.

Then as you grew older you began to ignore or push back your tendency to ask questions, either because you were busy with something else, or felt it was the wrong time, or did not want to bother anyone or just let matters ride. Thus, little by little, your bump of curiosity was submerged and gradually forgotten.

But how about now? Why not reactivate your bump of curiosity? Begin to ask questions and do not be satisfied until you have the right answers. Stop taking life around you for granted. Start probing, searching, questioning, until you know how and why things happen as they do, until you can explain such matters to others as well. You can start this very moment, with this page, with such questions as: "What is type? What are letters? How did they originate?" This may lead you into strange fields, into the study of language from the earliest pictographs to modern teletypes.

Be sure, however, that in following your newly aroused bump of curiosity you do not turn it into a vice. Curiosity is a vice when it concerns itself only with the pursuit of idle gossip, with spying on people, with prying into their lives or with meddling in their affairs. It is a vice when it becomes the "itchy nose" or the "loose tongue" of a "busy-body" who takes delight in spreading tales and rumors.

Curiosity is a virtue when it is the healthy, wholesome spirit of inquiry, the love of and the search for knowledge. It is a virtue when it is the earnest desire to learn and to understand, when it is the untiring quest for the causes or the reasons why things happen and people behave, as they do.

Develop the inquiry habit and give it as much time as you can without disturbing your regular routine or activities. You will be amazed how quickly such quest will open doors to you and how many horizons will begin to stretch before you in all directions.

Watching a teakettle boil and being curious about the lid popping up and down led to the discovery of steam power. The question why friction held back a moving object led to the discovery of the brake and its many uses in our machine age. Curiosity about pitchblende emanations led to the discovery and the isolation of radium. Further quests into radioactivity brought the development of nuclear fission and the coming atomic age.

As a matter of record, every advancement and every development made by man through the ages began with someone's "bump of curiosity", with someone's desire to know how, why, when and what if . . .

Start asking questions about the things you do not understand, the things you take for granted. Let everything around you make you want to know the reason why it happens as it does.

For instance, why does an electric light begin to glow when you push a button in the wall? What is the sound barrier? What is gravitation? Why does water turn to steam when brought to a boil? What is an isotope? Who were the Incas and what were their marriage ceremonies? How do you define memory? What is a pylon? How does your body breathe? What happens when you yawn? What is Nylon or Dacron? How does your TV set transmit sound and images? What are the crosses of Mu? What is Ramadan? Who is Siva, the destroyer? Why are you able to read these lines and understand what you read? Why do you like or dislike certain foods? What is the origin of your family name?

Any one of these questions and hundreds of others like them can start you on a wondrous, engrossing hunt for the right answers and introduce you to new interests and strange exotic worlds.

Start now. Start with your special interests, with the things you like or want to learn. Your local librarian or the various bureaus at Washington will readily supply you with lists of books or reference volumes with which to follow through on any subject you selected, and in many instances classes are available, under adult education auspices, without any charge.

Start with your preferences. You may be restricted or handicapped in one way or another but that should not discourage you because there are so many fields you can choose from, so many things you can do.

Take music, for instance. What a tremendous field it is! It embraces every step of man's march through the ages and is as big and broad as life itself. And nowadays with radio and TV broadcasts, with regular, Hi-Fi and stereophonic recordings and with excellent home-recording devices there is practically no limit to the ramifications that are available to you.

You may choose symphonic music or certain instruments in their ensemble. You may prefer choral pieces or chamber music. You may decide to select certain artists, composers or special periods in musical history. You may go for operas, folk tunes, hymns, jazz, rock-and-roll or sentimental ballads. The choice is up to you.

Perhaps your curiosity veers toward painting, handicrafts or the sciences. Whatever your leanings might be you can follow them at home or somewhere nearby, in your spare time or whatever time you wish to *give* to them, at little or no cost to you.

Do you like to work with your hands and handle parts, tools, brushes, food, flowers, books, clothing or living things? Parts may cover anything from a miniature mainspring to a giant crane. Tools may refer to a woodcarver's chisel or to intricate electronic installations. Brushes may suggest paintings or interior decorations. Foods may deal with cooking or planning meals. Flowers may have reference to growing them or arranging them. Books may have to do with writing, printing or selling them, and handling living things may go the entire range from animals to selling to teaching in accredited schools.

Do you lean more toward creative work? Then the entire range of inventive genius lies before you, to improve something already in use or to discover, develop or invent something totally new and different.

Are you given to strange dreams? Put them down on paper or tell others about them. Perhaps they can be translated into tales of wonder and awaken someone else's creative or inventive genius. Dreams are the steps to reality.

Do your dreams have plots and twists of fancy? Then perhaps they can be turned into plays or stories. Do your dreams have a tonal value? If so, perhaps they can be turned into melodies or symphonies, even though you do not know a single tune and cannot play an instrument.

Do you have an habitual lazy streak and always look for short cuts? Then, by all means, turn that tendency into creative channels. Most of our modern time-saving, step-saving and effort-saving inventions are the direct result of someone's streak of laziness.

Are you light on your feet and have a natural sense of rhythm? Then dancing is the field for you. It is surprising how much fun and satisfaction you can derive from teaching others how to dance or to join merry couples on a dance floor, for your personal pleasure.

Do you like to talk? Are you good at explaining things? Then, teaching may appeal to you. On the other hand, if you like to talk and are not too good at it you can take up public speaking at your local night schools, at no cost to you, and thus open new contacts and new opportunities for yourself.

Do you like to sing? Even if you are up in years and do not know one note from another you can still join a singing group and learn to carry a tune. Or, if there is no suitable group available, you can start one of your own, by bringing a few people together, engaging a teacher, and thus help yourself and others to spend many enjoyable hours in song.

Are you a lover of nature? Then why not join your local Audubon or horticultural society or some other congenial group that likes to commune with nature in all of its myriad forms.

These are but a few of the avenues open to you to follow your particular bent or inclination and add immeasurably to your joys of daily living.

Of course, you may have grandiose ambitions far beyond your means, your abilities or capacities. But if they are too impractical or unattainable for you let them go. Turn to the next best thing, in keeping with your age, your background, your environment and your potentialities.

Then, whatever it be, give it your wholehearted attention, imbue it with the fires of your desire, strengthen it with all the fervor and zeal that you can generate, and there at your finger tips will be your own Aladdin's lamp to turn each passing day into another jewel, for you to hold, to cherish, and to enjoy in the days yet to come.

The Tenth Hour

HOW TO OPEN YOUR EYES AND EARS

Do YOU WEAR mental eye blinders, see only what you want or have learned to see, and fail to notice and appreciate the big, wide, wonderful world around you? Do you wear mental earmuffs, hear only what you want or were taught to hear, and miss many of the tuneful melodies around you?

Those mental blocks or "shut-offs" hurt you in two ways. 1st. They make you accept the things you see and hear only in line with your set views and interpret them only in keeping with your preconceived notions and ideas. 2nd. They limit your views, narrow your vision, restrict your enjoyments and tend to entrench within you set beliefs, convictions and even prejudices.

None are so blind as those who refuse to see, either because they are not observant, do not know how to look, are disinterested or deliberately ignore what they see. None are so deaf as those who do not hear, either because they have not been taught or trained themselves to listen or because they refuse to listen and pay heed to what they hear.

Have you ever tried to see things with your eyes closed? Have you ever listened without hearing a single sound? If not, wondrous sights and tunes await you . . .

Nature in its myriad forms is teeming with sights and sounds and constant changes. The animate and inanimate life around you is ever-moving, ever-following its stipulated course as it begins and completes its cycle of birth, growth and eventual death.

You do not have to be a scholar, a student, a scientist or a naturalist to see, to hear, to notice, to discover, to enjoy and to appreciate the beauty, the mystery, the majesty and the intensity of life at your very doorstep.

If you live near an ocean or within a short driving distance from it, you can spend countless hours at its shores to look, listen and enjoy the sights. The waves rushing shoreward with a tumultuous roar, booming, thundering and sweeping everything to the shore. The white caps prancing gleefully atop the waves, skipping playfully from one crest to another, scattering foam and froth in all directions and finally losing themselves on the sandy beach.

You can watch the seagulls and hear their shrill calls as they rise, fall, bank, spiral and plummet downward into the roaring surf to grab an unwary fish. You can see them soar upward in ever-changing patterns of motion-in-flight as if playing merry games with the waves, the water, the currents of air and vying one with the other in sharp ascents and descents.

Even the seashells on the beach have a wondrous story to tell in their peculiar shapes, sizes, colors and intricacy of design as you try to visualize the former life within them. And, when the day nears its end you can see the setting sun spread a shimmering blanket of colors upon the glistening waters, in all the hues of the rainbow. You can watch the colors merge and mingle and change as the sun rides lower and lower to seek its resting place through the coming night, beyond the far horizon.

How far removed are those tranquilizing sights from the common humdrum of the ordinary day! How refreshing and stimulating in the midst of human artificialities! How uplifting in the sense of the infinite majesty it imparts to us!

Do you recall the days when as a child you used to lie on the grass, face upward, and see towers, spires, mountains, castles and warriors in the clouds scurrying by? Can you recall the peace you enjoyed, the dreams you dreamt, the future you envisioned for yourself while watching the clouds drift by? Would you like to relive the same joyous moments? Then hike yourself to the nearest window, open it wide and turn your gaze upward, to the azure sky and to the clouds passing by. Better still, get outside onto the nearest patch of grass, stretch out with your face upward and let memory take you back to the days of old.

Lie there supine and watch the clouds scurrying by. Of what do they remind you? If you could see faces, forms and figures in them years ago why not look for them now? Recapture the old wondrous thrill, rediscover the freshness and the imagery of your childhood days, reawaken the youthful dreams, and soon you will find that in some mysterious fashion peace will come to you and many of your present-day fears and worries will vanish in the thin air. It matters not how old you are now and how many summers have passed since you stretched out fully, lazily, upon the grass. The beauty and the wonder and the invigorating majesty of those days is still there, in the clouds over your head, and you can re-capture them . . .

Have you ever opened your ears to the song of the wind as it rushes through a street or a garden, as it blows around a bush or a tree, as it whistles through the leaves or the branches and chases odds and ends from the ground? Have you ever listened to the whisper of trees at night as they gossip about what they saw or heard or did, during the day?

Have you ever watched birds playing games or chasing each other with a swish, a swoop and a swirl? Have you ever felt the soft caress of a faint breeze or tasted a drop of fresh rain as it fell from the heavens and touched your face? Have you ever seen a flower open its petals wide to the warming sun and then nod gently in a gesture of thankfulness?

Have you ever gotten up with the sun and watched its rising beams chase away the shadows of the night? Have you ever seen a spider spin its delicate web with unerring precision? Have you ever watched a cat do its morning ablutions with infinite grace? Have you ever listened to the silvery peal of a child's happy laugh-ter or felt the caress of his casual, trusting touch?

Have you let love invade your heart and sharpen your eyes and ears to its untold sights and sounds? Have you ever felt the warm-ing glow of a friend's look and basked in the light of his sympathy and understanding? Have you ever given of yourself freely, whole-heartedly, to someone less fortunate than you, and sensed rather than heard his thankfulness and gratefulness?

It is surprising how much you can learn to see with eyes closed and how many tunes you can hear without a single note being played. The greatness of many poets, painters, writers, dramatists and accomplished speakers lies in their ability to see and to hear in many ways.

They have trained themselves to see with their ears and their minds and their hearts as well as their eyes. They have learned to listen and hear sounds inaudible to the ear. They have learned to notice striking differences in similarities and close relationships between dissimilar things.

You cannot read a single poem by Longfellow or several lines from any of Shakespeare's works, to mention only two writers, without encountering a score or more of striking similes and metaphors. This is true of all who have learned to see with an inner eye and hear from within. You, too, can cultivate that ability by developing your powers of observation, by learning to look for apt contrasts and comparisons, and by exerting the necessary effort to find the right words to describe what you are trying to convey.

And these are some of the ways to improve your sensory impressions:

ist. Give your full attention to what you are looking at, so that you could form a sharp, clear-cut picture of it, both visually and mentally, and let it linger with you until the impression is deepened.

2nd. Supplement the original sense imprint by using the other senses to implement it. For instance, a color combination aside from its complementary or contrasting hues may also impress you as being soft or loud, bold or subdued, cool or warm, intimate or impersonal, appropriate or discordant.

3rd. Compare or contrast the impression, mentally, with something else in its literal, figurative or associative aspect. In other words, look for likely similes or metaphors which would amplify or intensify the difference or the similarity.

4th. Connect the sense impression you received with something that you know, that will serve as a tie-in, that will help you to implant it, to recognize it, and to recall it later in detail.

5th. Form the habit of evaluating the things you see and hear as they reach your senses, even if the subject matter does not interest you at the moment.

6th. Try to see things with your eyes closed as if what appeared before you has been a single camera shot and recreate the imprint on your mental screen, in every detail.

7th. Try to listen to something you have heard as if the tune or the melody or the sound is reaching you through your sense of sight or of touch or through some inner vibration which has no auditory facility.

8th. Visualize what you have heard or seen not only as it applies to the immediate need, time, place or circumstance, but also how it would appear under totally different occasions or conditions.

9th. Practice to describe as accurately and as vividly as possible the things you have heard and seen. Look for words which give an exact picture of what you saw and heard.

10th. Try to understand as well as know what you are looking at or listening to, at the moment. If things are not clear ask questions or look for the explanatory details as soon as you have the chance.

11th. Describe something you have seen or heard as best as you can. Do it on paper for yourself and then compare your description with that of a poet, a writer or a dramatist. Note especially how he finds similarities in dissimilar things and how he utilizes picture words to paint a vivid picture.

Words are only symbols and unless you choose them carefully you may give people the wrong impression. For instance, supposing you wanted to describe a woman who impressed you favorably. You could say that she was lovely, charming, shapely, seductive, dainty, intriguing, exotic, captivating, delicate, sensuous, bewitching, stunning, provocative, radiant, interesting, alluring, comely, wholesome, curvaceous, motherly, matronly, cuddlesome, easy on the eyes, etc. Each adjective paints a different picture and hardly more than two or three can apply to the same woman.

12th. Take a direct interest or assume it is important to you and the things you see or hear will impress you more and stay with you.

Keep in mind this salient fact, the impressions you get from your sensory perceptions are not always the same. They hardly ever affect you in the same way or to the same degree at all times. Your feelings and emotions as well as the time, the place, the occasion and the circumstances may be different. Thus, it is highly possible that what you liked and enjoyed seeing, hearing, touching or tasting yesterday or only a short while ago may not appeal to you now. It may even displease you or upset you.

Open your heart and your mind as well as your eyes and ears to the world around you. Learn to see as well as to look, to listen as well as to hear, to contrast as well as to associate, and you will add many joys and pleasures to your daily life.

The Eleventh Hour

HOW TO ADD TO YOUR ENJOYMENTS

WOULD YOU LIKE to get more joy out of daily living even though there are many disturbing and disquieting things to worry you, to irritate you and to make it most difficult for you to enjoy life.

There are always things to displease you. Life can never be as smooth and bright, as good and pleasant, as you plan it or want it to be. And, it is so easy to grow discouraged, to find fault with people and things, to indulge in self-pity and to feel sorry for yourself.

Begin to grumble or complain, in a jocular mood, about some trivial thing, about the weather or your family, about your age or your looks, about your occupation or surroundings, about the world situation or your neighbor's dog, continue your grumbling or complaining for a while in the same light vein and soon the jocular aspect of it will be gone to be replaced by true irritation and resentment.

As a matter of fact, you can instigate or simulate any feeling or emotion and by maintaining the pretense long enough turn the simulation into the real thing. Psychologists contend that you cannot have a single deep emotional experience, real or imaginary, which does not reflect itself in corresponding physical manifestation.

Simulate anger or distaste long enough and it will turn into genuine anger or disgust. Pretend you are cheerful, sing or dance or whistle or laugh and soon your sadness will be gone. Visualize tempting favorite dishes vividly enough and before long your mouth will begin to "water". Take some trivial thing to heart, fume and fret about it over and over again and soon even a semblance of a similar situation will arouse the same fretfulness.

Our poets and writers have often stressed the fact that you cannot truly know the joys of pleasure until you have known pain and sorrow, that you cannot appreciate the exhilaration of freedom until you have been forcibly deprived of your liberty, for a while.

Be it as it may, having reached your present age and status, you surely had your share of "ups" and "downs", your joys and your sorrows, your triumphs and defeats, your moments of bliss and keen disappointment, and need hardly have more troubles to enjoy the good things in life.

But, to be able to derive more enjoyment from life about you, you have to develop that aptitude and cultivate that state of mind. Enjoyment is either a spontaneous or an induced feeling of delight, of pleasure, of satisfaction or gratification. It calls for an inborn or an acquired mental attitude which may or may not be influenced by the time, the place, the occasion, the circumstance or the people involved.

You may be one of a group participating in the same activity, partaking of the same food, watching the same performance, witnessing the same event or sharing the same contact and experience. Yet, you may be enjoying it immensely and others may not. What is more, you may derive enjoyment from it at one time and none at any other time. This may be due not so much to the time, the place or the circumstances but to your mood of the moment, to your emotional state or to the people with you and around you.

Some of us can derive a good measure of enjoyment from the little and simple things of life, others must reach a certain emotional pitch before they can begin to enjoy themselves. Some of us have to labor at developing a taste or a sense of appreciation while others seem to be endowed with the ability to get quickly into the proper mood and derive joy and pleasure in everything around them.

Such people have the innate or the developed knack of being able to inject a touch of play, humor, pretense, anticipation or play acting into any chore, task or situation before them. This tends to lighten their job and to brighten their task. It minimizes fatigue, reduces boredom, prevents exhaustion and increases the sense of enjoyment.

You, too, can acquire that fortunate ability. It will take a certain amount of effort and practice, but it can be done if you put your mind to it and back it with real desire.

Look for enjoyment in everything that you do or plan to do, but do not put a price tag on it and do not let the love of money, in itself, restrict you or dictate arbitrary terms to you. It is important, of course, to stay within your means and not go overboard on any projected enjoyment, but at the same time it is desirable to consider the differences involved. At times, a difference of only five percent in the total costs involved may be enough to change an otherwise dull, drab, dreary trip or event into a memorable, outstanding, highly enjoyable affair.

Some people deny themselves all the joys of living today in the fond hope of catching up tomorrow. They are waiting until the children are married, or the bills are all paid, or some rich relative passes away or until their retirement checks begin rolling in. But, unfortunately for them, the right time never comes. New bills, cares or responsibilities crop up, new delays hold them back and by the time they feel they are ready for it, old age or sickness or something else catch up with them and it is too late to look for enjoyment.

Do not short-change yourself. Do not put off living. Try to get some fun and pleasure today—now. There are so many ways to go about it, and you do not have to be young, good-looking, influential, well educated or well heeled.

But, be sure to take into consideration, your age, your economic status, your environment, your capacities and the time or the opportunities at your disposal. Try to fit those restrictions into your scheme of living while looking for and cultivating joys and pleasures within the framework of such limitations.

For instance, if you are "carving" your future now, you can gain satisfaction and gratification in carrying on your education, in mastering your trade or profession, in working and striving for the better days to come. If you are raising a family, derive your joys and pleasure from watching and helping your children get the proper foothold in their near future. If you have no children you can take enjoyment in your nieces or nephews or in helping some orphan or wayward child. If you are a grandparent you can have double pleasures from your children and their progeny.

Each age has its own particular joys and pleasures as time stamps its special marks upon your likes, dislikes, interests and preferences. Yet, within each stage of life certain basic values and possibilities remain and most of the small, simple, wholesome, everyday joys are within your reach.

Perhaps the greatest motivating force you can find to help you add to your enjoyments of life, at any age, is to have a set urge, a goal, an incentive, something in which you can fully believe. Make sure, however, to differentiate between the true inner urge and the mere desire to gain fame, fortune and acclaim. Make sure to separate the day-dreaming and the wish-thinking from the real inner drive which cannot be stopped or denied.

You may have to look for your goal or belief and once found work hard at it, by training yourself to overcome the old inertia and preparing yourself to face hardships along the way. Or, you may have already set your objectives and need no outside prompting or help on how to go about it.

You may be one of those hardy, dedicated souls who will keep on going against all odds, who will never give up trying, striving, pushing steadily ahead, no matter how far or impossible the goal. Or, you may be an average person, who does not want to set the world afire, who has no special talents or ambitions, who is just looking for simple ways to live and enjoy his life.

If you belong to the latter group, here are some of the ways to go about adding to your enjoyments:

1st. Learn to take life a little easier, with less push, drive or intensity, and try to derive your pleasures from whatever happens to be at hand, in the small, simple things of life.

2nd. Learn to overlook petty annoyances and inconveniences. Face your problems and meet your responsibilities as they arise, without rancor, resentment, dramatic or undue lamentations.

3rd. Learn to pay less attention to your own little troubles and be less sensitive about your occasional pains and discomforts. Above all stop crying or complaining about them to others.

4th. Learn to subordinate your personal wishes and preferences to the common good of others, especially when you are in company, and do not emphasize your displeasure or dissatisfaction.

5th. Learn to be more amenable to change and try to adapt yourself, as quickly and as easily as you can, to the new conditions and circumstances which are inevitable and which you cannot possibly change.

6th. Learn to face reality and stop running away from it. That never solves anything. Find a way to go on, meeting conditions as they are, without complaints or resentments.

7th. Learn to set aside your preconceived notions and beliefs, for the time being, especially if you are one of a group and want to be part of the crowd, or else seek other company.

8th. Learn to give of yourself more readily and let it be noticeable in your manner and in your actions. Try to add an extra smile, an extra kind word or an extra pat on the back to make others feel better and thus lend a warming glow to your own well-being.

9th. Learn to control your emotions and hold your anger in check. It may be a relief to show temper, to talk back, to put someone in his place but there are other ways to have your way, with less wear and tear on yourself and all concerned, especially if you do not want to burn your bridges behind you.

10th. Learn to cultivate a healthier outlook toward life in general and the people with whom you come in contact in particular. Be more tolerant, more forgiving and more appreciative. Let bygones be bygones. Do not drag in the past to plague you or the future to worry you. Give yourself a chance, and if need be, make a new start every day.

Follow some of these ways in your search for new joys and pleasures and you will surely find them day after day and hour after hour, as you continue your steady climb upward on your stairway to success and happiness, only nineteen space hours away.

The Twelfth Hour

HOW TO KEEP YOUR MIND OPEN

How QUICK ARE YOU to express indignation when others fail to follow your lead? How quickly do you assume the role of the aggrieved one and hasten to berate those who oppose you? How quick are you to show your resentment and begin to attack, accuse or condemn without any regard for the other person's feelings and without considering all the circumstances?

You may be able to impress a few people with your self-imposed importance and be successful in bullying a few timid souls to follow you blindly. But most people resent a domineering, dictatorial attitude, and he who practices it finds himself with very few friends, as he travels a rocky, lonely road through life.

If others do not see things your way or feel as you do or oppose your plans and ideas it is not because they do not like you or want to cross you. Their opposition may be due to one or more of these reasons:

1st. You did not express yourself clearly enough and they do not understand you. 2nd. Your "take-it-or-leave-it" attitude arouses natural opposition and resentment. 3rd. You may be taking many things for granted and your premise is false. 4th. You may be too close to the subject matter and cannot evaluate the full import or effect. 5th. They may know of conditions or circumstances which affect the plan or idea adversely. 6th. They have other suggestions in mind which could conceivably be better than yours.

7th. Their contacts, knowledge or experience differs from yours and they cannot see things in the same light, or in the same way, because no two people see and think exactly alike.

In a word association test conducted some time ago among psychology students the instructor asked his class to jot down the very first word that came to their mind after he gave them a single noun. He chose the word "father" and among the replies he received were, "mother", "husband", "job", "wages", "duty", "home", "children", "marriage", "hospital", "work", "bills", "poor man", and "father of our country".

If a single word can evoke so many different associations and connotations, how can you expect anyone to think and react exactly as you do and follow your lead implicitly, at all times? How can you assume the attitude that there is only one interpretation to whatever you say or mean to convey?

There are and there always will be differences in opinion, belief and reaction on every topic and on every subject, whether or not it touches us or affects us in one way or another. Make allowances for such differences and give others as much consideration as you would expect them to give to your views and ideas.

In other words, if you want to put over an idea and have people follow your lead, try to get over the other side of the fence for a while, try to see things with the other person's eyes before you become abusive or belligerent and begin to insist that your way is the one and only way.

The first step in cultivating an open mind is to set aside your self-justifying attitude and use the same measuring yardstick on yourself which you use for others. Try to see and to evaluate your traits, manners, habits, mannerisms, characteristics and general mode of behavior as you judge them, like them or dislike them in others.

For instance, if the other fellow is set in his ways do you call him headstrong or obstinate; but if you stick to your views and opinions do you think of them as firmness of character? When he expresses himself in a bold, vigorous, positive way, do you call it being biased, aggressive or opinionated; but when you do it, is it being frank, direct or outspoken?

When he takes time to think things over before saying or doing anything do you call it being slow or cumbersome; but when you stop to weigh all angles before reaching a decision do you call it being careful, deliberate or particular? When he acts on the spur of the moment do you say that he is impulsive, impetuous or irresponsible; but when you act in a similar way do you call it being alert, ardent or quick-thinking? When he is finicky or selective do you say that he is cranky or churlish; but when you pick and choose do you call it being discerning or discriminating?

When he is pleasant and amenable do you think of it as being servile or obsequious; but when you extend yourself and try to be agreeable do you call it being friendly or accommodating? When he is helpful and does things for people do you say that he is looking for honors or commendations; but when you help others do you call it being kind or considerate?

When he is mindful of the dollar and puts something aside for a rainy day do you call it being niggardly or parsimonious; but when you keep within a set budget do you want people to commend you for being thrifty, frugal or economical? When he guards his health and avoids jeopardizing his welfare do you call him a self-complacent, self-pampering person; but when you do it do you consider it smart, sensible or practical?

In other words, do you use an entirely different measuring yardstick for others than you do for yourself? Are you quick to criticize and disapprove of the habits and the behavior of other people and just as quick to justify, condone or even commend similar shortcomings in your own conduct and behavior?

Perhaps you have been looking at the different ends of the same telescope in so far as you and others are concerned. Perhaps you have been playing down your own faults. Perhaps you blind yourself to your failings or disregard your shortcomings while looking for perfection in others and insisting that they accept you at your own assumed and totally inaccurate valuation.

To have an open mind you have to take off the blinders of smugness, of self-justification, of assumed perfection and infallibility. Begin to judge yourself on the same basis and with the same measuring yardstick you use for others. And, if anyone should disapprove of something you do or say, do not look upon it as a catastrophe. Maybe he is right and maybe it is advisable that you change your ways or opinion on some controversial issue.

The narrow-minded person is usually an egotist. He may be good and kind, fair and considerate, in some respects but not on matters upon which he has already taken a stand. That is where he remains adamant and refuses to make the slightest allowance lest he be proven wrong and made to "lose face". He has to retain the feeling that he cannot be wrong and by refusing to accept any deviation fondly believes that it makes him infallible.

Such attitude, however, is hardly conducive to popularity and amicable relationships. It always awakens opposition and arouses resentment. Of course, it is commendable to take a stand upon certain matters and assume a positive attitude at times but be sure to differentiate between argumentation and outright stubborn pugnacity.

Be willing to change with the times, the need, the new conditions or circumstances, and do not be afraid of such change even if it contradicts everything you said, thought or did previously.

Change is the very substance of natural life. Nothing ever remains static or stationary. There is a continual process of change in you and all around you, a state of being born and disintegrating, of growing and maturing, of living and dying. All the animate and inanimate life in nature follows this constant change just as surely as day follows day and time stretches into infinity. You are no exception to this rule and the sooner you learn to abide by it the better for you and for your peace of mind.

This day is not the same as the day before or the day that follows, and whatever be the changes accept them as they come. "Joy and pain will come and go, in that you are not alone; hope and desire ebb and flow, as time fleets on and on".

Petrus Joubert, the statesman, said in part: "We should always keep a corner of our heads open and free so that we may have room for the views and opinions of our friends. Then we shall have heart and head hospitality . . ."

Go it a few steps further. Leave your mind open at all times, without reservations or prejudices. Make allowances for and respect the opinions of all with whom you come in contact day after day, and then you will surely gain in friendship, in high regard, in pleasures and in happiness.

The Thirteenth Hour

HOW TO MAKE "TODAY" COUNT

THE CHINESE PHILOSOPHER who first used the phrase "It is later than you think" is lost in antiquity, but that hardly matters for the moment. The underlying thought is just as valid and true today. Time is ever on the move. A moment once gone is beyond recall, and therefore it IS later than we think.

Perhaps one of the reasons why your life is not as bright as you want it to be lies in the fact that you fret too much about what happened yesterday, about what could possibly happen today and what could conceivably happen tomorrow.

In his inimitable manner Shakespeare had Caesar say: "Cowards die many times before their death . . ." What did he mean by it? Simply this, the coward frets and worries so much about the possible contingencies, sees himself dying in so many agonizing ways, suffers the pain and the anguish of so many different deaths that he dies a thousand times before his death comes. In a way, this may be true of you. You regret so much what might have been and worry so much about what could be that you have little or no time left to live today.

You forget that yesterday is gone with all the thousands of other yesterdays. No power on earth can bring it back or recapture a single moment of it. And so, whatever happened yesterday, whether or not some of it was due to your making, is already gone as irrevocably as time itself.

As for tomorrow, it is completely hidden from you and this

may be for the best. Thus, whatever tomorrow might bring has to bide its time and neither you nor any power on earth can change or affect it.

Hence, you have only today. It may be the only day in which you can do the things you want to do. So—make the best of it. Do not fritter away those precious hours in surmises, in regrets or in promises to yourself that tomorrow or on the next day you will start living and enjoying life.

How well Abraham Cowley, the English poet, put it:

> *Today is ours; what do we fear?*
> *Today is ours; we have it here.*
> *Let's treat it kindly, that it may*
> *Wish, at least, with us to stay.*
> *Let's banish business, banish sorrow;*
> *To the Gods belongs tomorrow.*

Learn to shut out the unpleasant things of yesterday, ignore the probabilities of tomorrow and do your very best today. Then, and only then, will you be taking one of the most important steps upward in your steady climb to happiness.

Of course you should utilize the knowledge and the experience you gained yesterday to improve the conditions of today. You should try to remember the mistakes of yesterday and not repeat them today. You should also plan for a better tomorrow on the basis of what you learned from this day and the day before. But beyond these sensible precautions hold on to every precious moment today and enjoy it. Use it to intensify your pleasures, to gratify the inner urge, to satisfy your sense of accomplishment, your well-being.

David Starr Jordan had this in mind when he wrote: "Today is your day and mine, the only day we have, the day in which we play our part. What this part may signify in the great whole we may not understand. But we are here to play it and now is the time. This we know; it is a part of action not of whining. It is a part of love not cynicism. It is for us to express love in terms of human helpfulness".

Omar Khayyam also had it in mind when he wrote:

> *Tomorrow's fate, though thou be wise,*
> *Thou canst not tell nor yet surmise;*
> *Pass, therefore, not today in vain,*
> *For it will never come again.*

And not to be outdone here is how Henry Longfellow put the same thoughts into a memorable poem:

> I *shot an arrow into the air,*
> *It fell to earth, I know not where;*
> *For so swiftly it flew, the sight*
> *Could not follow it in its flight.*
> *I breathed a song into the air,*
> *It fell to earth, I knew not where*
> *For who has sight so keen and strong*
> *That it can follow the flight of a song.*
> *Long, long afterwards, in an oak,*
> *I found the arrow, still unbroke;*
> *And the song, from beginning to end,*
> *I found again, in the heart of a friend.*

Surely, there is something in what Longfellow wrote, in spreading cheerfulness, friendliness and helpfulness as we go about the labors of the day. Who knows when or how the bread you cast upon the waters shall come back to you.

The way you utilize time today will determine the good you will get or the bad which you will perpetuate, for there is a good and a bad side to your character, your attitudes, your mental state, your general behavior and even to your physical appearance.

For instance, and this may be news to you, the two halves of your face do not match and are not exactly alike. The left profile differs from the right. One is finer, nicer, more delicate and refined than the other. As a matter of fact, if special composite photographs were made of two left or two right profiles of your face the difference would be so marked that you would hardly recognize your own face.

This fact is well known among artists, actors and photographers. And, it is a common practice among certain movie stars to employ private cameramen who have studied the star's face, who have carefully evaluated its good and bad sides and know exactly which profile is to be used in close-ups and which needs special lighting effects to offset its irregularities.

There is a good and a bad side to our actions and reactions. In the "Strange Case of Dr. Jekyll and Mr. Hyde", Robert Louis Stevenson fictionalized the fact that good and evil live side by side within us, and when evil is allowed to dominate it subjugates the good and before long becomes the indisputable master.

There are two sides to our character and most of us are fairly good at pretense and play-acting. A grouchy, grumpy, self-centered and short-tempered person can be kind, gentle, gracious, affable and self-effacing, when he wants to "put his best foot forward", when he considers such action profitable or wants to impress someone important to him.

Such pretense is quite common. We speak of it as "using company manners", or as "putting up a front" and although we know it is pretense we accept it, for the time being, at face value. This is due mainly to the fact that gentleness, graciousness, gallantry, affability and hospitality are highly emphatic and we are quick to respond to empathy.

There is a good and an evil side to thought. There is positive and constructive thinking or negative and destructive thinking. Your mind has absolute control over your mental and physical well-being. It can make you the sickliest and most miserable creature or the healthiest and happiest person alive.

It is all in how you think, in how you feel, in how you act and in how you build up emotional responses. You can think yourself into sickness, get all the symptoms of a given ailment and suffer all of its pains and agonies, even though there is not the slightest physiological reason for it.

This type of sickness, called psychosomatic, is quite common nowadays. The older you grow and the more you allow yourself to fall prey to emotional disturbances the greater your receptivity for and your likelihood to become sick, psychosomatically.

Sad and miserable would your life be if it were not possible for you to direct, to change or to influence, your thinking and thus retain the right, the ability and the power to make of your life what you want it to be.

Start your better, brighter life with generating bright, positive, inspiring and uplifting thoughts. Believe in and strive for the innate goodness of your being. Refuse to be deeply affected by petty annoyances and inconveniences. Harbor no ill-feelings or hatreds unnecessarily. Discourage the tendency to nurture grudges, grievances or resentments. Leave no room in your mind for gloom, despair or dejection.

All of these tend to build up negative emotional blocks. They are the forerunners of hypertension and can lead to such ailments as arthritis, neuritis, peptic ulcers, asthma, diabetes and heart trouble. These nervous tensions and emotional blocks can also lead to the sudden inability to be able to talk, to walk, to see, to hear, to feel, to use your hands or to remember.

These physical disabilities, called "symbolic conversions", occur quite often. They respond occasionally to medications but in most instances require lengthy psychiatric treatment, to be cured.

Cultivate positive thinking. Keep your eyes on the sunny side of life. Fill your mind with happy, cheerful thoughts. This does not imply that you should ignore reality, refuse to face facts, assume a Pollyanna attitude and pretend that everything is good, bright, fine and wonderful.

It implies only that you should not wallow in gloom or misery and take everything to heart. It calls for living normally, sensibly, naturally, accepting the inevitable, seeing life and conditions in their true perspective free from emotional overtones, connotations, implications and interpretations. Life is difficult enough as it is without complicating matters needlessly.

Stevenson personified your good and bad side in his "Dr. Jekyll and Mr. Hyde". These exact opposites live side by side within you and you are the one, the only one, who decides which shall have the rights in your daily life.

Begin your better, brighter and happier living by being good to yourself. Know what affects you adversely and guard against it. If you are allergic to certain foods, drinks or associations do not allow them to affect you.

For instance, certain sports or activities may be too strenuous for you or too excitable for you. In following them mainly to satisfy your whim or to show a stubborn streak you may be building up tensions or irritations harmful to you. They may not be noticeable for the time being but you will surely have to pay a heavy price later and the question you should ask yourself is— "AM I willing to pay the price?"

Some of your old-time habits may be harmful to you. You know it and yet you allow them to dominate you. You forget to remember that nature is basically selfish, that it always punishes those who ignore the simple, common-sense rules for sane, healthy living.

Know your capacities and limitations. Do not break faith with yourself and punish your physical and nervous system needlessly. Do not continue abusing yourself with the promise of correction or relaxation later on. Do not labor under the mistaken notion that all you need to make life happy is fame, fortune and acclaim.

They who drive themselves continually to achieve those ends and are cheerfully sacrificing their health, well-being and mental equilibrium are surely short-changing themselves over and over again. They are chasing a will-of-the-wisp, an empty dream, a false God, because by the time they reach their goal they can no longer enjoy life.

To paraphrase a familiar verse:

> *Man wastes his health with might and main*
> *His fame and fortune to attain;*
> *And then he spends his wealth again*
> *Seeking his lost health to regain.*

If you are driving yourself too much, stop to ask "Why?". Is it because you feel you have to keep up with someone else? Is it because you must follow him or else be left behind? Is it because you have to be richer than others and thus impress them more?

Are you under the impression that money or position is the only standard of measurement? Are you worshiping a golden calf? Do you attribute special attributes to those who amass worldly goods and none to yourself? Do titles or badges of office make you feel inferior or subservient? Do you consider the so-called "successful" men infallible and superior to you in every respect?

How foolish it is! How fallacious to underrate and underestimate yourself! Meekness and humility may be admirable traits but do not confuse them with self-effacement and debasement. Put a price upon yourself and do not drop it needlessly.

Have you ever had the chance to stand in the wings of a theatre and see the performers before the curtain goes up? Have you noticed how they suddenly square their shoulders, "paint" a theatrical smile on their lips and assume a gay, breezy front, although only moments before they were visibly shaken and unnerved?

This is true of all of us. We all tremble and hesitate before facing others and often "paint on" smiles beforehand. Even the greatest among us have their doubts, fears, failings and moments of indecision.

So—refuse to be awed by appearances or feel inferior to those who put up a big front. Respect your own sincere feelings and trust the true promptings of your heart. Of course, you will make mistakes at times but that is to be expected. Be ready to admit such mistakes and try not to repeat them.

You have many points in your favor in having reached your present status. You are a parent, a neighbor, a friend, a member of a community, and you have your spheres of influence among those who know you, like you and want to be with you. So—square your shoulders, put a theatrical smile on your lips, if necessary, and face the world with self-esteem and self-assurance. Then, surprisingly enough, others will begin to accept you at your valuation and want to follow or imitate you.

The Fourteenth Hour

HOW TO BANISH INNER CONFLICTS

THE OLD SPIRITUAL "Nobody Knows the Troubles I've Seen" could typify the chronic complainer that he knows nothing but trouble. As he puts it, he was singled out for punishment and fate is always against him. Bad luck "dogs" his footsteps and "bad breaks" stalk him wherever he goes and in whatever he does.

Strangely enough, a resume of his troubles appears to substantiate his claims that he has more than his share of mishap and misfortune. But stranger still is the fact that he attracts trouble because in many instances it is of his own making.

Unlike Typhoid Mary who continued to infect others with the deadly typhoid germs while remaining immune to them, such individual is the "jinx" not only to those close to him or around him but also to himself. He usually bears the brunt of the pain, the losses, the trouble or the punishment. He is no sooner out of one mess of trouble or misfortune than he is immediately plunged into another.

There are reasons for it because nothing happens of itself. When a man cannot hold down a job, is involved in frequent accidents, is at odds with his friends and family, fails to get along with people or has too many things go wrong for him time after time, the trouble can usually be traced back to him, to his general attitude, his customary behavior or habitual frame of mind.

Psychologists contend that such individual is "accident prone", a "maker" of troubles. He is careless, indifferent, thoughtless and deliberately rash or reckless. He is a misfit in whatever he undertakes and fails miserably at it because he has not learned how and does not care to know how to adapt himself to the need and the occasion.

He always has a chip on his shoulder, is oversensitive or over-critical. He feels the world owes him everything and when it is not delivered to him on a platter grows abusive, defiant, irritative, belligerent, intolerant and demanding. He is constantly at war with himself and carries his inner conflicts along in every contact with others.

Back of it may be (1) a masochistic tendency, (2) a desire to shift and escape responsibility, or (3) a compulsion for self-punishment.

In the first case, the complainer casts himself in the role of a martyr, of an unfortunate, much-maligned person who is being constantly punished for the sins of others. Yet, in the privacy of his heart, he glories in his troubles and enjoys his miseries. He feels that they set him aside from all the rest. They bolster his ego and feed his self-importance. However, he is usually so wrapped up in his own interests, so busy being dissatisfied with his lot that he develops a bad case of nerves and becomes a neurotic.

In the second instance, the chronic complainer usually magnifies his woes, intensifies his miseries and enlarges upon his troubles while bemoaning his seeming inability to cope with them. His tales are filled with anguish, with his resignation to his bad luck and unfortunate life and with his repeated attempts to counteract his mishaps and misfortunes. These accounts serve their basic purpose. They invoke pity, arouse sympathy, vindicate his appeal for help, promote assistance, shift his burdens onto others and enable him to escape his own obligations and responsibilities.

In the third instance, there is the desire to be punished and thereby pay for a real or fancied feeling of guilt. The guilt may be true, justifiable pricks of conscience or a strong urge to compensate, in some measure, for a wrong or a failing. The guilt may be due to repressed amoral desires, to former underhanded business dealings, to some temporarily concealed reprehensible act or to a breakdown in moral, marital or religious standards. The person seeking punishment may or may not be aware of the real reasons for his feeling of guilt but his compulsion may be just as strong and compelling.

Whatever be the reasons for your inner conflicts, never fail to remember that you cannot possibly run away or "bury" yourself anywhere because "you" and the "self" are inseparable. You cannot leave your "self" anywhere, at any time. Like your shadow it is always with you and the only way to get away from its customary influence is to effect changes within you.

Psychologists maintain that action begets feeling, that by simulating a given emotion we often generate the attendant feeling. In other words, if you pretend to be happy and cheerful when you are not; if you sing, dance, whistle, laugh or indulge in some humorous activity, even when it is play-acting on your part, it tends to generate a cheerful mood and by the same token weakens or dissipates gloom, sadness and depression.

Some people are always grumbling, fuming, fretting, sputtering or complaining. They are ever ready to put the blame for their failings or incapacities upon the times or conditions or just their bad luck. They steep themselves in unhappy contingencies and worry themselves sick about things which could conceivably happen but hardly ever do. They embrace the doctrine of fatalism in its worst implication, hardly realizing that fatalism has its stabilizing and bright aspects.

The old Greek conception of fatalism was that fate stands behind the gods and exercises the controlling power over us. Hence nothing can change or affect its inexorable course. The Mohammedan belief in fatalism regards all things, big and small, as unconditionally and unequivocally predetermined by the cosmic powers, so that nothing can possibly happen of itself.

The true fatalist is serene, tranquil. He never worries or gets into a flurry. To him "what has to be will be" is a law, a certainty. He knows he can do nothing to change whatever has to happen and so he accepts whatever befalls him with a stolid equilibrium and adjusts himself as best as he can to the new conditions.

Analysts and psychiatrists dealing with mental illness and emotional instability refute the fatalistic theory of everything being predestined but readily agree that nothing happens of itself. There is always a cause, an underlying reason, a contributing factor, although for the time being such may not be visible or explainable.

They claim, and you know it, that you contribute in a large

measure to your problems and conflicts because many of them are of your own making. They also contend, and you know it, that you can lessen your fears, diminish your anxieties and minimize your conflicts. However, the mere knowledge of these facts is not enough.

Your personal problems and conflicts have to be attacked from within, through gradual disruptions, deliberate substitutions, the removal of irritants, the change in mental attitude and the exposure to the light of day.

Some of your conflicts may have their origin in your upbringing, in the stringent social and religious taboos of your home environment which sought to deny and disregard all your libidinous impulses by the simple process of forbidding them. Those numerous "thou shall not's" disavowed completely all your base urges and amoral tendencies on the grounds that they were wicked, sinful and immoral.

But, an implied, an assumed or a seemingly enforced denial of its presence cannot dissipate amoral thought or carnal desire any more than the promise of a sumptuous meal hours or days later can assuage your immediate hunger. The only way to "displace" libidinous impulses is to divert them into new channels and translate them into other forms of interest and activity, or else they will become imbedded in the unconscious to gather explosive power and later emerge as a complex, fixation or neurosis.

One of the chief aims of the modern analyst is to bring repressions out into the open. The patient is encouraged to talk freely about himself and his grievances, about his hatreds and resentments, about his anxieties and frustrations. His vocal outpourings become a form of release and often reveal the fallacy and the absurdity of his inner conflicts. Thus, when exposed to the light of day they lose their power, lend themselves to "sublimation" or to "transference" and are thereby gradually debilitated.

Unfortunately, many of us cannot avail ourselves of the services of an analyst or a psychiatrist and have to help ourselves as best as we can. This is where it becomes essential for us to begin looking inwardly and learn why we are confronted with inner conflicts.

You may not be able to meet and resolve all of your problems or conflicts, because some of them may require competent analytical treatment. Yet, it is safe to say, that you can help yourself in a number of ways because you can minimize your troubles by following one or more of these suggestions:

1st. Try to learn where your conflicts start. If they have to do with your work find out how and why. Perhaps you resent the idea of working for others and it finds expression in arguments and dissension with everyone concerned. Perhaps you dislike the work you are doing and the resentments built up within you make you restless, careless, indifferent or disinterested in the duties or obligations you assumed and that, in turn, leads to misunderstandings and antagonisms between you and all others concerned. Perhaps the surroundings or the people with whom you have to work annoy you, upset you, irritate you and you cannot help but snap back at everything and everybody who gets in your way. If that is the source of your troubles, change firms or jobs, and the sooner the better for your nervous system and your well-being.

2nd. Discuss your problems and conflicts with a friend or with someone in whom you can put your trust. The mere talking about them may serve as a catharsis. You will "get things off your chest" and somehow it will lighten your load, release your tensions and make you feel better. Your listener may not be able to give you direct material help, but he may see things in a different light and suggest ways to cope with the situation. Sometimes his mere expression of sympathy and understanding, his encouraging words or his promise to stand by you in case of need may be enough to give you the extra "lift" or "push" you need to meet and "resolve" your problem and dissipate your conflict.

3rd. Check into your gut feeling. If you know you suffer from a feeling of guilt sit down with yourself and look into the reasons why you feel as you do. Probe deeply into the contributory causes and face the facts squarely, honestly, realistically.

Bring the reasons out into the open. If your guilt stems from shady business dealings, improper acts or immoral conduct your course is clear. Correct your wrongdoings, amend your ways, stop whatever you are supposed to stop and take steps to prevent any recurrence. Then, your guilt feeling will disappear and with it your conflicts will be gone.

4th. Change your mental aspects. The way you think, feel and visualize things has a marked effect upon your actions and reactions. The more you fret or worry about a certain possible contingency the deeper grows your anxiety. You are faced with problems and have to make decisions day after day. Whether you do right or wrong is not as important as your willingness to "take things in your stride", to shoulder your burdens and not to allow yourself to become a weakling or a neurotic. Stop pitying yourself or feeling sorry for yourself. Stop bewailing your set-backs and dramatizing your disappointments. It only aggravates the existing troubles or discomforts and tends to intensify your misery and unhappiness.

5th. Let time take its course. Many of your problems and conflicts stem from suppositions about what might happen. You may be building up mental hazards which will never come to pass. As a matter of fact, many a problem which appears insoluble has a way of solving itself as time goes by without your help or intervention, while others loom big and forbidding only because they look that way to you. Such problems can be compared to a sharp upgrade along the road which appears very steep and precipitous from the distance but as you come nearer it levels off, loses its sharp slope and you find yourself climbing the grade with ease.

6th. Start facing life realistically. Stop getting upset about trivialities and petty annoyances. Act your age and do not behave like a temperamental movie star. No one has to bow or kowtow to you or pay special attention to you. Do not set yourself up as someone better than those around you and assume imperious airs. It will not endear you to anyone and is bound to bring you heartache and misery.

7th. Stop finding fault with people and belittling or criticizing everything they do because it does not coincide with your notions and ideas, with your beliefs or preferences. Cultivate a sense of fairness, of tolerance and understanding. Give people the benefit of the doubt. It will stop many a possible conflict before it starts. If you made a mistake admit it and try to correct it. If someone else erred in some way do not bring down heaven and earth on him. Look for extenuating circumstances and give him a second chance. He, in turn, will do the same for you.

8th. Make comparisons. Compare what you gain with what you lose and evaluate the good with the bad. Many a problem is not as serious as you take it to be and many a change is often for the better. It is surprising how a so-called "bad turn" can become a step upward in position, in contacts, in chances and in opportunities.

9th. Emphasize the good and bright side of what is going to happen. One way is to "make light" of it or "take it on the chin" as it were; another way is to minimize the effect or the inconvenience and pack the situation into as small a place as possible; still another way is to dwell upon the advantages to be gained and become enthused about the new possibilities. The popular song about the man who complained and was disheartened because he had no new shoes until he met someone who had no feet voices a sound and healthy outlook upon set-backs, handicaps, hardships and occasional disappointments.

10th. Refuse to take yourself too seriously or ascribe special importance to what you say, do or think. What if others do not accept your plans or ideas so readily? What if someone else's idea is better than yours? What is so tragic about having to step back a pace or two at one time or another? No one is perfect and no one is infallible. Nothing is so bad that it could not be worse and no situation can be totally unbearable as long as you have the will, the spirit, the urge and the determination to go on.

11th. Start doing things for others, even if it means only your presence, your words of encouragement or your expressed offer to help along. Nothing tends to banish personal trouble and disparage inner conflicts any faster and nothing brings you a quicker sense of goodness and inner satisfaction than when you do something for others, especially those less fortunate than you.

12th. Turn to God for strength and guidance with an abiding faith in His omnipotence. Many a weighty problem and a deep inner conflict seems to evaporate in the thin air when we turn to God with a simple and sincere prayer, for prayer has the strange power of lifting us out of ourselves and our troubles.

Whatever be your inner burden a prayer from the heart is sure to help. It will brighten your spirit and give you the hope, the strength, the courage you need to go on. Learn to carry prayer into all of your tasks and peace will be with you throughout the day. Follow some of these suggestions conscientiously. Let them guide you, inspire you. Then many of your conflicts will vanish as you go steadily ahead, onward and upward, higher and higher, on your stairway to success and happiness, only sixteen space hours away.

The Fifteenth Hour

HOW TO OVERCOME AN INFERIORITY COMPLEX

FOURTEEN DAYS have passed since you began the climb on your private stairway to success and happiness. You have gone up fourteen steps, covered fourteen hours in time and space, and have reached the second landing, the halfway station. Now you can look down as well as look back with justifiable pride.

If you climbed one step at a time, took to heart the suggestions given and made every effort to follow through, you are no longer the same personality who started a fortnight ago. You left part of your old "self" behind and now, while you pause for a breathing spell, take stock of your gains.

You reviewed old concepts and gained new ones. You have a better appreciation of your potentialities and a greater respect for the power of habit. You know, now, the importance of the right mental attitude, the bad effects of losing one's temper and the cumulative values of using spare time. You know now how to deal with inner conflicts, how to counteract the middle-age let-down and how to add to your enjoyments. All of this should make you feel proud of your advancement and give you the urge to go on and on.

Now it is time for you to take another important step. Remember, however, that you may run into an occasional leveling-off period when you will appear to be standing still. If such be the case today, tomorrow or at any other time, do not let it discourage you. Those lulls are transitory. They come and go and the momentum you lose for the time being can be quickly regained.

Consider now the ways of how to overcome your lack of self-confidence, your sense of being inadequate, your feeling of inferiority, that is assuming you have that problem. This is primarily an emotional condition, an induced frame of mind, and as such can be modified or nullified by you.

When Dr. Alfred Adler coined the term "inferiority complex" he used the phrase to denote sets of emotional ideas centered upon real or imaginary handicaps. He also used it to indicate the attempt on the part of an individual to compensate for his feeling of inadequacy with behavior intended to prove such feeling unjustified. Since then, the term "inferiority complex" has been used loosely for any form of misbehavior.

How would you define an inferiority complex? Do you have one? Ask these questions of yourself and you will be able to tell. 1. Do you feel unequal to or beneath those with whom you usually associate at work, at play or elsewhere? 2. Do you undertake tasks or responsibilities beyond your means or abilities just to remain in the good graces of someone? 3. Do you let people abuse you, mistreat you or walk all over you because you are too meek or submissive? 4. Are you awed by names or titles, by badges of office or assumed authority and would do most anything to ingratiate yourself with so-called "big shots"? 5. Do you consider yourself an outsider or an interloper in the midst of certain people? 6. Do you feel you have to be obsequious or subservient to be accepted? 7. Do you demean or debase yourself unnecessarily? 8. Do you follow unquestionably anyone who takes the lead, even though you know he is misleading you? 9. Are you afraid to take a stand or to voice an opinion because someone may not like it? 10. Are you forever apologizing for something you said or did, when there is no call for it?

If your answer to one or more of these questions is in the affirmative you have an inferiority complex and should take steps to be rid of it.

Some people go about it in the wrong way. Take the case of Will Bryden. You may know him under another name. He has charm, ability, personality and could go far in business and social circles but he "loves" to argue. He is always "itching" to start an argument and will argue about anything under the sun, just for the "heck" of it. Once started he will not budge an inch, no matter how wrong he might be in his premise, claims or contentions. If he cannot gain the upper hand with direct arguments he uses innuendoes, raillery, sharp words or any other means to discredit his opponent and thus usually wins by default. As a result the people who know him shun him like the plague and refuse to discuss anything with him.

Or take the case of Sheila Sommers. You may know someone like her. She is a sensible, level-headed woman in every other respect but not in her clothes selections and in her make-ups. That is where she displays the oddest and strangest quirks. When the occasion calls for street wear or party wear she shows up in slacks and sweaters, and when informal clothing is expected she appears in low-cut semi-formal or formal wear with heavy show-time make-up. She uses the strangest color combinations and when it comes to bags, accessories or costume jewelry the more comment she can create with her choice the better she likes it.

Bert Anderson, he could be your neighbor or associate, who is sensible in every other way, shows his strange quirk in his hair-dos. For months at a time he sports a "butch" or "crew-cut" type of hair cut, then takes a sudden dislike to barbering and lets his hair grow and grow like an abandoned patch of grass. Or, for weeks at a time he wears side-burns or nurtures a dandy mustache and then just as suddenly discards them and shaves twice a day to make sure he is clean-shaven.

Mona Steiner, who could be one of your friends, just likes to talk and once started can hardly ever be stopped. When she is warned not to monopolize every conversation she is quick to assure you that such is not the case and proceeds to prove it by giving numerous reasons why, without interrupting herself, that is not so.

Rita Amherst, and someone in your family may remind you of her, is a modest, reserved and well-mannered woman. But her laugh grates on everybody. It is a sharp, shrill, strident clarion call with blaring overtones that carry it far and wide. No matter where she might be, her laugh is a clamoring discordant shout for all to hear, to shrink from and to comment upon with displeasure.

What is behind such odd behavior? Psychologists say it is a cover-up for a feeling of insecurity, for an inferiority complex. It is the desire to catch and hold attention and thus bolster one's ego. It is also the shout of defiance, the unconscious expression of belligerence or inner resentments. It is a defense mechanism intended to compensate for the feeling of inferiority.

But odd, bizarre and questionable behavior is not the way to offset an inferiority complex. It is only a mask, a poor substitute for gaining attention or interest. It can never engender respect, sympathy, regard, confidence or friendship.

Look for the underlying reasons and counteract their influence upon you in one or more of these twelve ways:

1st. If your inferiority stems from the company you keep, stop associating with all those who make you feel small, inadequate or insecure of your place and position. Stop following the pretenders, the climbers, the "show-offs", the wastrels and the self-styled leaders. Stay on the safe side and cultivate the company of those who live normally, sensibly, within their means and their abilities. It will be better, healthier and more enjoyable for you.

2nd. If the contributory causes to your feeling of inferiority are in the tasks you undertake at work, at play or at social functions, stop accepting them. Avoid placing yourself in a position where you might appear in a poor light or find yourself in waters beyond your depth. Know your limitations and the extent of your abilities. Refuse to become involved in anything that you cannot follow through successfully just because it puts you in the limelight for a while or because you want to ingratiate yourself with somebody.

3rd. If people with names, titles, badges of honor or with "money to waste" make you feel small, self-conscious and insignificant avoid close contact with them. Why play "second fiddle" to them? Why be the "stranger" at their table, the "outsider" at their gatherings? Seek your own level, among those who come nearer to your standards and those who make you feel comfortable.

4th. Place a price on yourself, on your knowledge, ability, dignity and self-respect. Do not demean or debase yourself needlessly. Refuse to serve as a mat for others to walk upon. Voice your displeasure, your likes or dislikes, and never sell yourself short.

5th. If you consider yourself an outsider or an interloper with certain people there may be a sound reason for it. You do not belong there. It is commendable to seek higher levels but only when you have prepared yourself and not at the expense of your self-esteem and self-confidence.

6th. If you want to look well and dissipate your feeling of inferiority stay within your bounds and do not overreach yourself. Find out what you can do best, work diligently at it until you excel in it and then capitalize upon it. People will be quick to notice it and to appreciate it, and thus in turn will help you to combat your inferiority complex.

7th. Sell yourself on the fact that you are as good, as capable, as important and even better in some respects, as those with whom you usually associate. Take your right place among them and do not steep yourself in needless doubts and apprehensions.

8th. If your inferiority stems from oversensitivity or self-consciousness it may be due to the fact that you take yourself too seriously and attach too much importance to what you say or do. No one expects you to be perfect and not make a mistake now and then. Do not labor under the assumption that people have you on their minds and talk constantly about you. This is not the case. Rid yourself of these notions and your self-consciousness will gradually disappear.

9th. If you feel that you are not liked or wanted or welcomed when you come in company it may be due to the fact that you expect too much. Perhaps you ask for too much interest or attention. Perhaps you wear your heart on your sleeve and feel hurt when people fail to notice it. Perhaps you are engrossed too much in your own interests and show too plainly your disinclination to talk about or to consider anything else.

10th. If you have been afraid to speak up, make up your mind to think your way through a given problem and come to a set decision. Then "stand by your guns" and fight for your right to feel as you do. Be adamant about that stand of yours, insist upon your right to express yourself as you have. Do it again and again and before long your fear of speaking up and your feeling of inferiority will be gone.

Of course, now and then, you may take the wrong attitude and expose yourself to censure or criticism. But do not let it dismay you or discourage you. You may swallow a little water and even sink at times, but you will rise to the surface and eventually get into the "swim" of things.

11th. If you intensely dislike what you are doing but keep at it halfheartedly because you are afraid to make a change you are doing an injustice to others and are unfair to yourself. Make the necessary changes. Strike out anew. Rid yourself of the fear that you cannot do any better. There is more to you than you give yourself credit for in your abilities and adaptabilities. You may meet with hardships for a while, in making the change, but eventually you will be better off and much happier.

12th. If you have been too willing to take "second best"; if whatever is offered to you is "good enough" for you; if you are forever apologizing for living or for taking up room, how can you expect others to accept you at a higher or a better valuation? You have definite values and potentialities which you, and you alone, can develop and capitalize upon. There is no one exactly like you anywhere in the world, and there is no reason why you should step back and assume you are not worthy of regard, consideration and appreciation.

There are differences within you which separate you from all the rest. Find out what they are and use them to advantage. They may be in your suppressed urges, in the things you always wanted to do but somehow never got around to them. Give voice to them —now! Work at them—now! But, do not delude yourself with the belief that the world will step aside to let you breeze by or that people will flock all around you to help you reach your secret wishes and desires. Your road ahead may be rough, steep and almost impassable, and fame or acclaim may never be yours, but go on, just the same.

You will gain strength in trying, in striving, in reaching out, in the mere effort of working at something you wanted to do. And somehow, as you hold on to your resolve, as you continue trying over and over again, your sense of inadequacy will vanish and your feeling of inferiority will disappear.

The Sixteenth Hour

HOW TO DISSIPATE FEAR

THE DICTIONARY DEFINES fear as alarm, dismay, anxiety, awe, reverence, fright or dread. Psychologists, however, see fear as a multifaced emotional process. It may express itself as doubt, distrust, suspicion or uncertainty. It may refer to the awareness or the expectation of danger, trouble, discomfort or displeasure and the desire to avoid or to escape bodily harm or pain. It may be expressive of trepidation, unrest, uneasiness or disquietude. It may lead to terror or to panic. It may have nothing to do with physical danger and be the build-up of premises, surmises, suppositions or unfounded apprehensions.

Your mental reaction to fear is the father to the physical preparation to fight, to run away, or to ward off, in some manner, the pending danger. It takes form in one or more of these ways. The knees tremble, the hands shake, the body perspires, the muscles grow tense, the glands pour more adrenalin into the blood stream.

the heart races, the liver works faster and the digestive system is slowed down or stopped by spasms. You get a sinking feeling in the pit of your stomach and all the usual normal bodily functions go haywire. This shock to the nervous system does not go by unheeded. Allow yourself to go through it needlessly a number of times and you will become a neurotic, a nervous wreck.

The pattern of a "fear behavior" goes through these stages. The perception or the awareness of the pending danger; the desire to fight it, to avoid or escape it; the bodily responses activated by the mental concept; the aroused disagreeable feelings or disturbed sensations; and, the search for relief, escape or safety. Find the way to offset or counteract anyone of these stages and the fear will disappear.

There are three general groups of fear and each has its particular impact and influence upon us. They are the beneficial fear, the justifiable fear and the fancied or imaginary fear.

The first fear is a blessing in disguise and adds to the goodness of life. The fear of God is the beginning of wisdom. The fear of hurting someone we love encourages care, esteem and solicitude. The fear of going hungry or becoming a public charge later in life encourages us to work, to strive and to save. The fear of being injured or killed on crowded highways promotes better driving and the observance of safety rules. The fear of contamination or sickness engenders cleanliness and methods of sanitation. The fear of lawlessness fosters social and civic codes and the necessary enforcement agencies.

The second type of fear is one of nature's safety signals. It directs your attention to an imminent peril to your life or to your safety. It warns you of possible danger and cautions you to seek safety or take the proper protective measures.

The third type of fear deals with imaginary situations and is indicative of a neurosis. For instance, if you are afraid of heavy traffic on a busy thoroughfare and take special precautions in driving or in crossing it on foot you have a justifiable fear and are doing the sensible thing. But, if you are afraid to use the sidewalks for the same reasons or cringe whenever you see a car approaching you it is a neurotic fear. Likewise, if you are afraid to swim in shark-infested waters, along some tropical shore, your fear is justi-fied but if you express the same fear about getting into a home or a public pool you have a definite phobia and need mental treat-ment.

Fear, worry, anxiety and apprehension are part and parcel of everyday living. We are afraid of pain and dread possible hos-pitalization. We are anxious to make good or worry about someone we love. We fret about our future or have apprehensions about a pending situation. We have doubts about something we did or did not do properly or are distrustful of someone's motives in giv-ing us advice. We feel uncertain of our position at a given time or are uneasy about the reaction of someone we want to impress. We envision trouble or danger ahead and lose courage in the midst of a set-back or build up suppositions about possible contingencies.

All of these are manifestations of fear. Some of them are minor and others more predominant. How about your fears?

Some of them may go back to your childhood days when your young, impressionable mind was influenced by many "don'ts". As a result, you grew up with an induced fear of the dark or of police-men, of crossing a street or climbing a stairway, of sleeping in a strange bed or taking a trip by yourself, of talking to strangers or going into the water, of voicing an opinion or of making a simple decision.

Some of your fears may go back to tensions built up over a period of time. They may be due to overwork, to undue strains, to lack of diversion, to the aftermath of physical exhaustion, to business worries, to strained relationships at work or at home or to other factors which keep you on edge.

Some of your fears may be based upon faulty teachings or hasty conclusions arrived at without consideration for the facts. For in-stance, you may have been warned about the danger of black-widow spiders and therefore developed a morbid fear of all spiders. Or, you know that many snakes are poisonous and are mortally afraid of all snakes, so that even the harmless garter snake starts you shaking and trembling in mounting fear. This list can be lengthened to include the fear of mice, cats, dogs, birds, bugs, thunder, lightning, open or closed places, high or low places, stairs, window panes, and even a visit to the dentist.

We manage to cope with some of our fears. Others, however, are transposed into introversions. The individual thus affected withdraws into himself. He grows highly self-conscious, anti-social, and gradually retreats into a private world all his own, where fantasy replaces reality. This becomes a psychosis and often leads to schizophrenia.

If your fear is already so deeply imbedded that you need psychiatric care it would be foolish to try to help yourself, but if it is still within your ability to analyze it and recognize it, here are a few ways in which you can dissipate it:

1. If there seems to be no basic reason for your fear other than an assumption, face it frankly, boldly, and turn it upon itself. Start with an act of will and do the very thing of which you are afraid. It might mean sleeping in the dark or using a strange bed, talking to a stranger or taking a walk at night, holding a cat or patting someone's dog, voicing an opinion or making a snap decision and sticking to it.

This deliberate act to "meet" an existing fear and "beat" it by doing what you are afraid of, is one of the simplest cures possible to take. Do such thing consciously, intentionally, several times in a row, and soon the old fear will be gone.

2. If your fear is based upon an emotional angle, upon anger, irritation, resentment or frustration, it may be helpful to swear or to shout, to cry or to laugh, to grumble or to complain, to bluster or to express yourself volubly, strongly, vigorously. It tends to blow off the emotional steam. Used in moderation it becomes a safety valve to release pent-up feeling. However, it is not recommended as an habitual way to be rid of an emotional fear.

3. If your fear is due to thwarted longings, to disillusionments or nurtured grievances talk to someone about them. Select a stranger rather than a close friend or a member of your family. Let him be the vessel into which you pour out your heart and your troubles, your fears and anxieties, your grudges and disappointments. Be frank with him, hold nothing back.

And, should you find yourself associating your confidante or analyst with your troubles or identifying him with your hatreds do not be dismayed by it. This "transference" is one of the curious twists in our nature. Yet, strangely enough, it is a form of release, because as you continue exposing your inner repressions before him the association with and the embodiment of your troubles will disappear and the healing process will begin.

4. If your fear is a hidden anxiety, a premonition, an inner warning or an ill-at-ease feeling, there may be a justifiable reason for it. It might pay you to check deeper into that impression. For instance, if you are contemplating changing your job, selling your home, disposing of your business, moving to a different city, ven turing into a new field or becoming associated with certain un familiar groups, the change-over may not be as good as you believed it to be. The risks may be too great, the time may not be right or something else needs closer check-up and examination.

5. If there seems to be no plausible reason for your fears try to trace them back to their beginning, in the full light of your present maturity. Fear shrinks from exposure and yours could very well be a carry-over from olden days, an accumulation of old resentments and emotional disturbances.

Look for a comfortable way to sit back or lie down and send your memory back through the years. Try to recall every little thing that discouraged you, nettled you or frightened you. Recreate the same situations, if possible, and you may find to your amazement that your present fears are the manifestation of childish concepts and hardly worthy of thought or consideration now. You were beholden to and dependent upon your parents and your elders at that time and were held back or were forced to abide by their whims, wishes and desires. But you are an adult now and the old parental rules and restrictions no longer apply to you. See those fears in that new light and they will surely disappear.

6. If you are beset by groundless fears try to list them on paper in all of their details. What are they? How and why do they affect you as they do? Is it because you are growing older and must slow down a bit? Is it because you cannot keep up the old pace or the people with whom you associate are too fast a crowd for you? Is it worries about a relative or a member of your family, for no

apparent reasons? Is it the anticipation of possible pain or dis-comfort? Whatever those fears may be put them down on paper and make it a point to compare and evaluate them from every angle. Perhaps the troubles or difficulties you envision are not as bad as they appear to be. Perhaps you are giving too much free rein to your imagination and are basing your assumptions on false premises.

7. If your fear is due to an emotional conflict, it may be some thing which you can correct without much difficulty. Maybe you have grown too impatient or impetuous of late and need a rest or a temporary change of pace. Maybe you are driving yourself too much and should take things a little slower, easier. Maybe you have grown too eager or ambitious lately and are putting too much of a strain on your nervous system. Perhaps a little diversion or a new interest or a change in outlook will tend to reduce the tension and thus give you the needed release from your fear.

8. Your fear might be dissipated if you were to follow the cus tom of pious Jews and were to throw it away, figuratively. During their High Holidays, on the first or the second day of the Jewish New Year, in late afternoon, pious Jews go to the nearest body of flowing water in order to follow the ritual of the "Tashlith", the "Throw-away". They come as close as possible to the edge of the running water, without wetting their shoes, and empty their pockets of the odds and ends placed there earlier, while reciting the special "Tashlith" prayer.

The belief and the symbolism implied in the "Tashlith" rite are, that just as the supplicants have emptied their pockets of impurities to be carried off by the running water without pollu-tion, so shall their hearts and their minds be fully emptied of fear, worry, anxiety and disappointment, beginning with that moment and carrying through for the balance of the year.

It is a laudable custom, and the Rabbis who first instituted the "Tashlith" rite had great vision and worldly understanding. You *can* empty your heart and mind of troubled thoughts and disquiet-ing feelings. You *can* minimize your fears and figuratively throw them away, day after day.

9. If your fear thrives on your mental attitude you can often effect a change by accepting a new belief or by cultivating a different outlook. And this story, adapted from the Talmud may be helpful to you.

A Medean king who was always kind, merciful and considerate, suddenly found himself beset by strange fears and recurring fits of temper and despondency. They grew worse from day to day and at the suggestion of his trusted advisers he appealed to King Solomon. Solomon agreed to help and after some contemplation ordered one of his silversmiths to fashion a signet ring with the letters "G", "Z" and "Y" etched upon its face.

When the ring was completed Solomon presented it to the King of Medes with these words: "I have had this ring made especially for you. Note the letters on its face. They are the initials of three Hebrew words, 'Gamm Zeh Yaabor', (This, too, shall pass). They are also the mystic call letters of three friendly spirits I imprisoned within the ring. Should you find yourself beset by worry or anxiety once again, gaze upon those letters, concentrate upon their double meaning and intone the three words, 'Gamm Zeh Yaabor' slowly, loudly, seven times. The imprisoned friendly spirits will then come to life, surround you with an aura of invisible but powerful protection, and your fears and anxieties will vanish in the air".

The Medean king took the ring and the advice to heart and from that day on was freed of his fears, worries, anxieties and apprehensions. You cannot invoke the aid of King Solomon for your troubles. Yet, in a way, you can utilize the same symbolism of the ring. Try it! Inscribe the mystic letters "G", "Z" and "Y" on a sheet of paper, hold it before you when you are troubled with fear, concentrate upon their double meaning and intone slowly, loudly, seven times "Gamm Zeh Yaabor!" Do it with the same assurance that the Medean king had and your fears will also disappear . . .

10. If your fear is due to conditions beyond your control and there is no way in which you can change them, nurturing a fear about them is not going to help you at all. It will only aggravate matters and intensify your troubles and discomforts.

The sensible way to deal with the matter is to accept the inevitable and do your best to live with it. Minimize its effects upon you as much as you can. Reduce the contributory factors as much as possible and change your ways, ideas, contacts or behavior so that the aggravating factors would be lessened.

Keep this salient fact in mind: your fears whatever their origin or the reasons behind them stem from within. They thrive on ignorance, on mistaken beliefs, on assumptions and on your mental acceptance of their power. They cannot grow or linger there where positive thinking is practiced and encouraged.

Fight fear with self-confidence and self-assurance. Fear feeds upon itself and grows fat with its own implications. Clarify doubt or suspicion as quickly as you can and do not nurture needless trepidations. Give groundless fear no chance to linger with you and it will seek other places in which to grow.

The suggested ways to resolve minor fears have helped others and should be helpful to you. So—adapt them to your needs and then, like the shadows of the night running before the beginning of the new day, your fears will run and disappear.

The Seventeenth Hour

HOW TO ELIMINATE NEEDLESS WORRY

WORRY IS another form of doubt, fear, distrust, uncertainty or uneasiness. The more you give in to it the better it thrives and the greater its influence on you. Strangely enough, most of your worries are of your own making. They are figments of your imagination, surmises and suppositions built around imaginary possibilities. You envision all sorts of contingencies and your imagination supplies the worrisome details. They magnify the probable effect, amplify the existing or the pending condition and intensify its importance or influence far beyond the actual facts.

Some people are chronic worriers. They can never see or hear anything without adding a touch of doubt or anxiety to it. They can never visualize or experience a given situation without attaching to it the possibility of trouble, mishap or displeasure. They always expect to meet with discomfort or disappointment and strange as it sounds their expectations often materialize.

They seem to have an affinity for trouble. Even in their daily contacts with others, at work, at home or at play, they manage to introduce an element of doubt, suspicion or hostility, and by arousing resentment become veritable "carriers of dissension" for themselves and for all with whom they associate.

It is normal and natural for us to have doubts and uncertainties, to go through various "ups" and "downs", to have moods of depression from time to time, to be irritated by conditions or circumstances, to be upset about something that happened. These things are part of life and need not worry you too much because they are transitory in character. It is only when your emotional distress persists, when worry becomes a habit, when you continue seeing only the sad and dark aspects of life, that you need give concern to it.

In other words, if you fret and fume about every little thing that happens; if you nurture doubts or uncertainties for no apparent reasons; if you let anxieties and apprehensions crowd you; if you allow worries to dominate you and influence your thoughts and your actions, you are building up a negative thought pattern, you are establishing worry as a prevailing mood or as a habitual behavior and you are doing great harm to yourself.

If your worries are still in the formative stage you can help yourself but if they have entrenched themselves and assumed a pattern of melancholy you are in trouble and need psychotherapy.

Psychologists maintain that depressive moods and many forms of emotional distress can often be dissipated in one or more of these ways:

1. By compensation. You look for ways to make up for the existing condition and develop or cultivate other compensating forms of interest, activity or expression.

2. By rationalization. You think of and align various reasons why the mood or the distress should not exist or bother you and thereby weaken its effects or influence upon you.

3. By projection. You attribute the reasons for the existing mood or condition to circumstances beyond your control, adapt yourself as best as you can to the seeming inevitability, and thereby relieve the bothersome, troublesome, worrisome condition.

4. By belittling. You minimize the effect of the mood or the condition by ridiculing or disparaging its importance. You build up the premise that it is hardly worth the price or the effort to be maintained and thus weaken its influence.

5. By recall. You trace the mood or the condition to its time or place of origin and by recalling its simple unwarranted begin ning can weaken and nullify its immediate accumulated effect.

6. By comparison. You compare the good with the bad, weigh one against the other, and in that light reconsider and reevaluate the condition or the circumstance which contributes to your mood or distress. This often dissipates the worry angle, lessens the impact of the depressive mood and counteracts its effect upon you.

Some of our sad, despondent or melancholic moods are often only a pretense, a hidden selfish desire to make others worry about us. Those moods are disguised attempts to gain sympathy, support or attention, and when allowed to linger grow very quickly and lead to mental aberrations.

One of the ways to minimize sadness, offset despondency and disperse melancholic tendencies, according to Dr. Alfred Adler, is to take an interest in others, especially those less fortunate than we are. The mere effort to bring relief, joy, help, pleasure or satisfaction to others is a palliative. It makes you forget your own troubles and buoys up your flagging spirits. It provides you with new incentives, promotes well-being, minimizes personal problems, gives you a satisfying inner glow and dissipates your disturbing, disquieting moods.

If you happen to feel sad, worried or depressed at this moment try this simple formula. Decide to cheer up and bring a smile to the lips of every person you meet for the next hour or two. Go out of your way, if necessary, to do something for somebody, something that will make him smile, that will elicit his thanks and appreciation. You will be surprised to note how quickly such action on your part will pay off and how someone else's pleasure and gratefulness will find a similar pleasing response in you. It matters not when or where you try it, the results will be the same.

Still another way to dispel a "low", depressive mood is to fill your mind with inspiring, uplifting thoughts. Here is one, a poetic version of the 23rd psalm, as written by George Herbert:

The God of Love my Shepherd is
And He that doth me feed;
While He is mine and I am His
What can I want or need!
He leads me to the tender grass
Where I both feed and rest;
Then to streams that gently pass,
In both I have the best.
Or if I stray He doth convert
And bring my mind in frame;
And all of this not for my desert
But for His holy name.
Yea, in Death's shady black abode
Well may I walk, nor fear,
For Thou art with me, and Thy rod
To guide, Thy staff to bear.
Nay, Thou dost make me sit and dine
Even in mine enemies[1] sight;
My head with oil, my cup with wine
Runs over day and night.
Surely Thy sweet and wondrous love
Shall measure all my days;
And as it never shall remove.
So neither shall my praise.

If you are worried about a given issue or problem face it in a normal, sensible fashion. Analyze it from every angle and consider its effects if it should pass, if it should remain as is or if it should grow more aggravating. Adapt yourself to the immediate situation and at the same time take the necessary steps to be prepared and to deal with matters should the situation become even more aggravating.' Thus, no matter what happens you will not be caught unaware and unprepared.

If the situation facing you is something beyond your ability to change or to control, and if its effects are permanent, what good will it do you to fret, to fume, to worry and to carry on? How far will it get you? Is it not better to accept the inevitable and do the best you can under the circumstances?

Supposing that through some misfortune, through a sickness or an accident, you were suddenly deprived of one of your senses or were to lose an important bodily organ and became handicapped. That would be a real calamity. It would tax your moral fiber, strain your energies, sap your strength and affect your outlook on life.

And yet, there are literally thousands of men and women, in all walks of life, who are blind, deaf, legless, armless or otherwise incapacitated by crippling ailments who triumphed over their physical handicaps and have not only made a place for themselves in the world around them but have also earned the respect and the admiration of all with whom they come in contact.

Some of those handicapped men and women gained fame and renown. Steinmetz, Schubert, Stevenson, Oscar Wilde, Alec Templeton, Helen Keller, Sarah Bernhardt, Lionel Barrymore, Franklin D. Roosevelt, to name but a few. They proved beyond any doubt that a physical disability cannot impair or affect latent capabilities and the unconquerable inner urge to find expression, satisfaction and gratification.

However, there are handicaps, of your own making, of a mental or behavioristic nature, that are more injurious and more damaging to your health, morale, happiness and peace of mind.

For instance, take the individual who is wrapped up only in himself; who tramples love, kindness, loyalty and friendship under foot; who disregards the rights and the sensibilities of others; who thinks only of his own gains and interests; who is forever on the run to amass more and more of worldly goods. Can he ever be happy, satisfied or contented? Of course not. He is more handicapped than the person who lost his sight, his hearing or the use of his legs.

Or take the person who is consumed by greed or envy, by suspicion or jealousy; or the one who is forever fighting the world and himself; or the one who is always pitying himself or is feeling sorry for himself or can never find anyone or anything to please him; or the one who is so set in his ways, so prejudiced in his opinions, so arbitrary in his decisions that he cannot get along with anybody. Such people are much more handicapped than one with a physical disability who has adapted himself to his limitations and is living a full, joyful life.

No man is an island or a retreat unto himself. Life affects us at every turn and we cannot keep out cares, worries, anxieties or obligations often thrust upon us by others or by conditions beyond our control.

That is where you must train yourself to live with the things or the conditions you cannot change. Such acceptance of the inevitable will relieve you of needless tension and prevent emotional disturbances. It will enable you to cope with and adjust yourself quicker and easier to the new situation. It may also uncover from deep within you hidden reserves of energy and stamina, of courage and resourcefulness, and strengthen you in the midst of adversity.

Examine each problem and each situation carefully. If you feel that it lends itself to change or modification check into all the angles. Learn how and why the situation came up. Look for the underlying reasons and contributing factors. Then try to eliminate them one by one and put this plan of operation to work as soon as you can, without undue trepidation or excess worry.

Excessive worry feeds upon itself. The more room you give it the faster it grows and the quicker it gets out of bounds. It is the devil's own brew and no matter how little of it you take it always generates fear, fosters uncertainty, breeds suspicion, upsets well-laid plans, spreads doubt, hampers decision and destroys confidence.

Worry clouds issues, befuddles thought, feeds on premises, adds to the confusion and weakens the will or the desire to go on. It saps your strength and has an adverse effect upon all bodily functions. Doctors and psychiatrists agree that worry is one of our worst enemies. It builds up hypertension and is responsible, in a large degree, for ulcers, diabetes, colitis, high blood pressure, skin disorders, digestive tract ailments, nervousness and heart disease.

Give worry no chance to linger with you. Close your mind and your heart to its crippling influences. The best way to offset it is to keep your mind and your hands busy doing something else. You cannot smile and sneer at the same time. You cannot cry and laugh at the same time. Likewise, you cannot be sad and glad or gloomy and cheerful at one and the same time. You can do each in turn, one before or after the other but never together.

These simple facts are the basis of modern occupational therapy used so effectively in mental institutions. Utilize the same idea. Leave no room for worry to linger in your thoughts and it will not stay. Look at the sunny and bright side of things and gloom or sadness will have no chance to affect you.

But, if you feel you must worry now and then, it might be a good idea to follow Norman Vincent Peale's formula on how to cure yourself of the worry habit:

"Resolve not to use the 'worry' implication or any of its synonyms. Substitute in its place a positive thought, indicative of hope, faith, courage, belief and confidence.

"Think of your worry habit as a tree which has to be cut down. You cannot handle it all at once but you can work at it in stages. Start chipping away at the lower and smaller branches first, then the upper ones, the top and finally the trunk itself. Do it gradually, consistently, and the task of removing your 'tree of worry' will become easy to handle.

"Set aside a special day in which to do all of your worrying. Promise yourself to give full time and attention to each and every worry which you have accumulated. In the meantime go ahead with your usual daily activities as if you did not have a single care or worry in the world. Finally when your 'day of worry* comes make an early start. Have a good breakfast, then retire to a room away from friends and members of your family, take out the list of worries you have marked down through the days that passed and begin worrying. Of course, you may find that many of your

erstwhile worries have grown strangely elusive while others have disappeared and vanished without a trace . . ."
This cure for worries brought out so beautifully by Peale in *The Power of Positive Thinking* may sound foolish to you but it is sound in principle and highly effective in application. When you are sure of yourself, when you are doing what you like to do, when you meet problems face to face, and feel that you are accepted and appreciated, worry cannot linger or bother you.

The Eighteenth Hour

HOW TO COMBAT FRUSTRATION

FRUSTRATIONS STEM from opposition to or interference with your urges, wishes, wants or desires, when someone or something blocks, holds up, thwarts, crosses, interferes or interrupts them, seemingly by purpose or design.

Frustration can stem from a number of sources. One of them can be dissatisfaction. For instance, if you are dissatisfied with your job or your family, with your business or social life, with your status or surroundings, with what you are and with what the future holds for you, it can be nurtured into resentments and turn into frustrations.

In so far as your line of work is concerned you spend considerable time at it. Hence, whatever be the field you follow, it affects your social standards, your contacts with others, your outlook and your way of life. If your work agrees with you, you adapt yourself quickly to everything about you. But if you are in constant conflict with what you do you carry it through in every other contact with people around you. Those conflicts pile up one atop the other and in so doing accumulate explosive power. You must take steps to divert them or else you will be in the midst of a mental breakdown.

If you cannot seem to get along with your superiors or co-workers on the job; if you get into arguments or disagreements with all concerned; if you hate the mere thought of going to work or staying at it, by all means make a change or else your built-up frustrations will turn you into a neurotic or a mental casualty.

The feeling of frustration differs from anger in the fact that it is not a sudden surge of anger or irritation followed by an immediate act of aggression but rather a slow, gradual growth of chagrin, displeasure or resentment leading to eventual reprisal.

Frustration can stem from your mental attitude toward your family, your friends, your economic status or the way in which you accept occasional set backs and disappointments. Some people and things rub you the wrong way. You cannot avoid them or discard them, and so you bite your lips to hold back your anger or resentment and add more and more to your frustrations.

Your eventual reprisal may be passive or violent in form, simple or involved in its action. It may become a direct act of aggression against the person, the plan, the condition or it may be deliberately hidden. It may be turned into direct assaults along many fronts wherever expedient or convenient, or it may take the devious route of starting false rumors, of instigating smear campaigns, of undermining confidence or of using other ways to disparage or discredit a given person, plan, motive, purpose or mode of operation.

One violent form of frustration in action is seen occasionally on our highways. A long line of cars is following a dawdling driver who "hogs" the road and gives no one a chance to pass him. The drivers behind him honk their horns but he does not budge and goes on as unconcerned as if he were the only one on the road. The line behind him grows longer and soon the anger, the impatience and the resentment build up into a frustration. One of the drivers behind the dawdler swerves sharply out of line to pass to the right of other cars or over the center line in spite of heavy oncoming traffic. Others follow suit and new traffic accidents are added to the growing list of mishaps.

Some frustrations turn inwardly and lead to introversion, to a retreat from normal living, to retrogression and even to attempted suicide. Other frustrations are transferred or displaced into wrong channels. They are directed against inanimate objects or against innocent people who happen to get into the way and are attacked and even injured without cause or warning.

A play recently shown on TV dealt with such form of frustration transference. The main character, the attorney for the defense, working on a personal injury case, was checking into the eyewitness accounts of the accident and ran into an amazing series of non-related contributory incidents.

The driver of the car deliberately hit the passing motorist because of a frustration held against his employer for being fired that morning without any cause. The employer felt exasperated because his wife abused and attacked him on the same morning, at the breakfast table, for no apparent reason. She was frustrated because a supposedly close friend snubbed her publicly the day before. That friend was upset because the snubbed one's husband refused to give an adequate amount to her pet charities.

He was disturbed because by handing him the wrong club earlier on the same day his caddy made him lose an important golf game. The caddy was frustrated because the court decision he counted upon was lost for him by the very same attorney who was investigating the accident. The attorney was upset because of a silly argument with his fiancee the night before. Thus, a simple misunderstanding between sweethearts started a series of events ending in a serious traffic injury to an innocent passer-by.

Fantastic as this fictional plot may appear it is based upon fact and could easily happen that way, even to you.

If you suffer from frustrations they may be due to one or more of these reasons:

1. Your childhood. Perhaps you were delegated to second place in favor of a brother or a sister, or subjected to rigid discipline, or thwarted in your simple wishes, or openly disliked and criti cized, and that built up your emotional disturbances.

2. Your early years. Perhaps you were an only child and were cuddled and pampered by over-indulgent parents. You always had your way with them and grew up expecting the rest of the world

to follow suit. But when those expectations failed to materialize you developed deep resentments and frustrations.

3. Your lack of training. Perhaps you were allowed to grow up like Topsy and were never trained or prepared for life. You lack self-reliance or self-confidence and cannot adapt yourself to a world so strange and forbidding to you. Hence you are on the defensive or embittered and that, in turn, brings many disappointments, resentments and frustrations.

4. Your general attitude. Perhaps you are so wrapped up in your own wishes, motives, interests and desires that you completely disregard the rights, the feelings and the sensibilities of those around you. This fosters animosities and breeds ever-growing re sentments and frustrations.

5. Your customary behavior. Perhaps you are a habitual fault finder who is never satisfied with people or things around him. This creates constant dissension and breeds frustrations.

There are other reasons why frustrations occur. Among them are physical or mental exhaustion, lack of interest or diversion, marital disunity, business worries, poor health or recurring disappointments.

Here are some of the ways to combat frustration:

1st. Know how a frustration works. It can be compared to steam generated by boiling water. Kept tightly sealed in a boiler the steam will build up terrific pressure and eventually cause an explosion, but directed properly and carried off gradually it will serve set purposes. Your frustration may begin with a peeve, a "slow burn", an irritation or a resentment allowed to linger. Hence, one of the ways to combat a growing frustration is to face it openly, normally, as soon as possible, before the gathering steam causes an explosion.

2nd. If the frustration is due to someone's actions a simple direct approach might eliminate the irritation. Bring it to such person's attention, without rancor or belligerence, without being officious or insolent, and as a rule the aggravation will be removed and your "steam" will escape slowly, quietly and harmlessly.

3rd. If there is no way to reach or to stop the offender, "gripe" about the irritation by giving voice to your resentment. Do it without involving your listeners and blow off the steam without adding fuel to your aroused resentment.

4th. If it is possible, try to remove the cause of the irritation. If that is not feasible make the best of the situation and try to minimize its effects upon you, until such time when you can get away from its influence.

5th. Dissipate the feeling or the assumption that whatever happens is a deliberate attempt on somebody's part to hurt you, thwart you or harm you. That is seldom the case. Never take such things as a personal affront and thereby work up a growing resentment.

6th. Transfer or displace your frustrations by directing your energies into new, wholesome channels which will tend to minimize the irritations and their effects upon you.

7th. Dissipate the tension or the aggressive phase of your frustration by taking an active part in sports or in other activities that will occupy your body and mind and leave no room for harboring needless resentments.

8th. Make light of the irritation or its underlying cause by ridiculing it, by exposing its fallaciousness, by dwelling upon its silly aspects, by rationalizing or by refusing to let it upset you.

9th. Write down all the details of the irritation on paper and put the paper aside for a while. Then, a few days later, reread your notes, have a laugh about them in the light of the new day and tear the sheet of paper to shreds. This often resolves a petty irritation.

The ways suggested may not apply to a deep frustration requiring competent analytical treatment. But in many cases these steps will be helpful to neutralize a resentment, to minimize a simple emotional irritation and eliminate a minor frustration.

The Nineteenth Hour

HOW TO LESSEN NERVOUS TENSION

As A MEMBER OF SOCIETY you have to restrain many of your amoral urges and atavistic impulses. In some instances, the home or the community, the social order and the law-enforcement agencies impose the various restrictions and the penalties for infringement. In other cases, it becomes your personal responsibility to follow and to abide by the established code and modes of behavior. The only ones who can do as they please, without being directly answerable for their actions, are infants and the mentally retarded or unbalanced.

Our actions and reactions are based upon habitual behavior and psychologists speak of four general behavior patterns:

1. The person who is authoritarian in character and sees only black and white with no gradations between. There is no middle road. You are either with him or against him. As a self-appointed leader he assumes a dictatorial attitude without any leeway for a difference in approach or viewpoint. He hides behind a blustering bellowing front when he is not sure of his ground. When he meets no opposition he becomes the swaggering bully, the demanding despot. Yet he is ever fearful lest someone stands up to him and calls his bluff and is therefore under constant tension.

2. The person who is self-centered and self-engrossed, to whom nothing else matters but his own welfare, comfort or benefit. He is usually so wrapped up in himself that he has no time to enjoy life because his greedy nature is never satisfied with what he al ready has. He is quick to drop friends, to trample love and loyalty under foot, and to use any and all means to gain his ends. He measures all people by his own yardstick and is therefore distrust-

ful of everybody. This tends to foster dissensions and animosities and keeps his nerves on edge.

3. The person who is subservient and submissive and readily follows anyone who assumes the lead. He is a will-o'-the-wisp and like the chameleon takes on the color of his immediate attachment and surroundings. He hardly ever has a mind of his own, is never sure of himself or his loyalties, is ever afraid lest he offend those whom he is following and is under tension most of the time.

4. The chronic fretter, fumer, bemoaner or complainer who is never satisfied with people, conditions or circumstances around him. He is always unhappy about something, always ready to find fault. This makes him irritable, tense, hard to live with and a burden even to himself.

The balanced person is one who has a little of each of these in his make-up, and fortunately he represents the majority of us. He is the average, normal, sensible individual who can take the lead or follow others, who looks out for his personal interests and welfare but at the same time is mindful of the rights of others. He takes care of his obligations, follows a customary routine at work and at play and is usually fair-minded and law-abiding.

If you belong to that majority you can cope with your day-by-day problems and manage to live a fair life. But, if you happen to have a preponderance of the characteristics of the four categories mentioned take steps to mend your ways and acquire a balanced personality.

Your personality is the reflection of what you are and what you appear to be. It is the sum total of your traits, characteristics and general behavior as evidenced by your expressions, actions and reactions. You can assume a given personality for a while, play a part as it were, and pretend to be someone entirely different from what you really are. But such pretense is short-lived and your true self reappears before long.

Tension comes from jumpy, jittery nerves and some of us are naturally nervous and high-strung. Some people are born with a nervous temperament. They are more active, sensitive and imaginative. This can be true even of twins or brothers and sisters raised under the same roof and under similar conditions, in education, upbringing and environment.

They may differ very little in general appearance or inclination, and yet one may have a nervous disposition and be unable to sit still for any length of time while the other may be a placid, phlegmatic, easy-going person. One may be quick to react, to feel hurt or become upset, to get into a sad or a happy mood and the other may have a thick skin and never be bothered by anything around him.

You have an intricate system of nerve networks which control your mental and physical functions. The lower system starts with your spinal cord, the other is grouped in a section of your head, at the beginning of the spinal ganglia, just above the base of your skull. The section consists of two halves, each the `ize of an average thumb, and is called the "interbrain" or the thalamus.

The thalamus oversees the proper coordination of all bodily activity. It controls the functions of your various organs, as well as the vascular, glandular and digestive systems. It regulates your blood pressure, your body's temperature and the proper balance of chemical substances in your blood. It colors, filters and instigates your thoughts, feelings, sentiments and emotions. It knows more about you than you can ever learn. It holds the driver's seat with you to make certain that your organism functions smoothly, properly, efficiently and almost automatically at all times.

Ordinarily, your thalamus knows its way about and seldom leads you astray. But conditions may arise when your driver becomes so confused and bewildered, so disturbed and disorganized, that he goes to pieces and you have a neurosis on your hands.

How does it happen? Why the confusion and the disintegration? A simple illustration may help you to understand. No doubt, you own a car, are a competent driver and feel equal to any traffic situation. But supposing you were on a main highway, traveling smoothly along, and were suddenly confronted by several traffic police and by a number of conflicting signs. One says, "Stop!", the other, "Keep Going!". One says, "Slow down!", the other, "Speed up!". One tells you to turn right, another points to the left and a third motions you to go straight ahead.

You do not know which command to obey. You try one and are bawled out for doing it. You try another and once again meet with a stern rebuff. Finally, you give up in disgust and stop "dead in your tracks".

The same confusion happens when your thalamus is confronted by conflicting emotions, one opposing the other. The collision between them and the demand of each to follow its dictate is totally bewildering. The thalamus tries to go both ways but that is impossible, and so the resultant deadlock stymies its response, deadens its abilities and forces it to go to pieces. The result is, a neurosis, a maladjustment, a derangement or a breakdown.

Nervous tension comes from severe shocks to the nerve cells. Sustained anger, nurtured grievances, emotional conflicts, intense worries or anxieties, physical exhaustion, repeated snarls with others at work or at home, deep seated resentments, imbedded animosity and piled-up frustrations, all of these build up nervous tension.

What are some of the ways to cope with and to deal with nervous tensions? Here are seven of them.

1st. If your tension is the result of worry, find out why you are worrying. If it is due to some inner warning, check into the contributory factors to learn why you feel as you do. Is something threatening your job, your home, your family, your contacts, your safety, your future or your community status? Are you laboring under an assumption or a mistaken belief? Are you worrying too much about possible contingencies that are too remote to be considered? Are you overemphasizing the actual conditions or over-estimating the possible consequences?

2nd. If your tension is due to a new condition or situation facing you, stop to consider all the advantages and disadvantages. Perhaps the benefits to be derived outweigh all the apparent shortcomings; perhaps a change in your usual routine or practices in keeping with the new conditions will be a decided improvement over the old. Perhaps you hate the change only because it is a departure from the old but the new plan, idea or condition is far more desirable and offers greater chances and opportunities. We are creatures of habit and hate to depart from the old and the tried, but the new may be so much better, in every way.

3rd. If your tension stems from a fear or an uncertainty the sooner you learn why it exists the quicker the solution. This may call only for a rearrangement of plans or procedures, of removing easy-to-get at irritants, of reestablishing self-confidence or assurance, of setting a set course of action, of clarifying a mistaken notion or of removing the doubt element. Whatever be the solution put it to work as soon as you can and the tension will be eliminated.

4th. Your tension may be due to the fact that you have undertaken tasks, duties or responsibilities that involve too many risks and are beyond your usual capacities. You know they may hurt you financially, socially or otherwise. You know they may have an adverse effect upon your job, your contacts, your future or your position and you hesitate to "own up" to your incapacity or inability because it might involve a "loss of face". And so, you are on edge and your tension grows from day to day. But, would you not be better off to stop before you get in deeper?

5th. Your tension may be due to the fact that you feel guilty, because you did something wrong and acted unwisely, or because you erred in judgment and made a mistake and people are sure to find it out. If this be the case then stand up now, as it were, and "face the music". Your admission is bound to be in your favor and will surely mitigate some of the damage done. At the same time it will lessen your sense of guilt and thereby remove or minimize the nervous tension.

6th. If your nervous tension is due to pending changes or new developments try to evaluate them as impartially as you can. You may be too close to them and cannot see them objectively. Perhaps you would do well to discuss their import and relationship to you with someone who does not have a direct, close, personal interest in the matter and can help you see it in its proper perspective. Perhaps all you need is a change in viewpoint, a new mental attitude.

7th. If your tension is due to self-effacement, to a feeling of inadequacy, look for ways to change it. Learn to respect your knowledge, ability and sense of perception. Believe in yourself, in what you do or represent. No one is going to place a higher valuation on you than you do. If you feel you know nothing and are a nobody, others will accept you on the same basis. This does not imply that you should put on airs and act the "big shot", but that you put a price on your dignity and self-respect. Your attitude toward yourself, in the privacy of your own heart, determines the attitude others will take toward you.

Have faith in your abilities, in your integrity, in your place and in your particular sphere of influence. Keep a sane sensible outlook upon life and people around you. Voice your thoughts when you are sure of yourself but hold your tongue when uncertain of yourself. Be chary with criticism and quick to praise, and before long you will be free of nervous tensions.

The Twentieth Hour

LEARN HOW TO RELAX

MEDICAL MEN, psychologists and psychiatrists, agree unanimously that many of our anxieties, frustrations, resentments, nervous tensions and resultant physical disorders would be minimized, and some of them completely forestalled or eliminated, if we were to learn how to relax.

It takes no special knowledge, aptitudes or preparations to learn how to relax and how to benefit by its soothing, healing and becalming influence. But, unfortunately, many of us are too busy chasing the ever-elusive pinnacle of material wealth to give much thought to our well-being and take time out to relax.

And so, we turn to stopgaps, to the temporary relief of opiates, barbiturates and tranquilizers. They serve their basic purpose at first, but before long they become a crutch, a necessity, a habitual need. And, as the system grows used to them we have to increase the dosage, or use them more often, and eventually we become mental casualties.

What IS relaxation? The dictionary defines it as the lessening of tension or restraint, the cessation of work or effort, the easing of strain, the indulgence in a pastime or a diversion. That is clear enough but the synonyms give us further clues of its values. To relax is to lighten, to reduce, to curtail or to modify; to submit, to comply, to slacken or to give way; to rest, to recline, to repose, to let go . . .

All of these refer to relaxation and have an important bearing upon our mental and physical well-being. We must take time out to rest, to repose, to replenish our energies or else we will go to pieces.

One of nature's ways to guard against complete physical and mental exhaustion is the need for sleep. Sleep is one of the most important metabolic functions essential to life but no one knows its exact nature. It is a complex process requiring close, harmonious cooperation between body and mind which cannot be ignored. It is nature's way to halt temporarily many of the normal sensory functions and overt muscular activities, thus providing needed rest and replenishing expended body energy.

Neurologists have been able to identify and to isolate two tiny areas in our brain, known as the reticular formation and the hypothalamus, which regulate our sleep and wakefulness. They go on to say that during sleep our brain continues work with a skeleton crew, intercepting and interpreting all incoming messages as usual. Most of the messages are side-tracked but those considered urgent or important are given priority and are rushed ahead to the control centers. The brain hastens to respond. We are awakened and hasten to take whatever action is needed to meet the situation.

Among those important messages may be a sudden unfamiliar noise, a baby's cry, a bodily need, a sense of danger, a call for help, a change in room temperature, an habitual hour for awakening or a conditioned response to certain stimuli.

It is possible for us to abstain from sleep for as many as forty-eight hours without apparent ill effect. However, tests show that if another similar period of sleeplessness follows the first in quick succession or if the period is extended beyond the original forty-eight hours there is a growing loss in sustained attentive ability. There is also a growing tendency to develop dizziness, headaches, burning eyes, nervousness, irritability and lightheadedness. There is also a growing dullness of perception, lack of awareness and marked sluggishness in normal reflex action.

Sleep is a "must" with all life including plants. Sleep promotes rest and relaxation under all conditions and circumstances. However, the amount of sleep required by a given individual is dependent upon his age, his work, his daily habits, his physical and psychological make-up.

The older or the less active person needs less sleep than someone else and need not worry if his average sleeping period is below the customary seven or eight hours. But, sleep is controllable by habit and one can teach himself to sleep longer than is needed.

In fact, sleep can become an opiate and be used as such by anyone who does not want to face his thoughts or his problems. It becomes his avenue of escape from consciousness. He tries to prolong his sleep as much as possible and if he cannot do it naturally he uses sleeping pills.

He wants to deaden his senses, to escape the coming of the new day with the problems or responsibilities of the day before still unsolved, and uses sleep as an "out". He woos sleep by staying in bed, by keeping out light and noise, by using pills, and manages to retain the semblance of being half-awake and half-asleep a great deal of the time. Of course, this "running away" does not solve his problems and eventually they reach a point of explosion which he cannot escape . . .

You may need seven or eight hours of uninterrupted sleep to be completely refreshed. Someone else, being of the same age, doing the same work and living under the same conditions, may need only six or seven hours of sleep and feel sluggish or languid if he stays in bed for a longer period of time. This is due to the natural differences in temperament and physiological make-up.

If you cannot sleep soundly and naturally during your customary sleeping hours or if you have trouble dropping off to sleep there are reasons for it. It may be due to pathological or to physiological insomnia. The first is usually the result of pain, infection, anemia, toxemia or organic diseases of a functional nature. The second may include one or more of the following reasons:

1. Too much food eaten just before going to bed with the di gestive process barely started or disturbed.

2. Worry about something that did or might happen, at work, at home or elsewhere.

3. Dwelling upon or reliving the business cares, the work prob lems or the unpleasant moments of the day just passed.

4. Overstimulation due to excess food, to drink or to late-eve ning festivities.

5. Having no regular hours for going to bed.

6. A stuffy or overheated room with little or no air circulation.

7. Too many covers or not enough of them to make lying in bed comfortable.

8. The fear of not being able to fall asleep.

9. Failure to let go of tensed muscles and being able to relax.

10. Reading too much while in bed or watching excitable TV shows too long, just before retiring.

11. Family quarrels, disagreements or other emotional disturb ances before going to bed.

12. Failure to shut out or eliminate noises, strong lights, bad odors or other disturbing sensory impressions.

Any one of these or a combination of two or more may affect you and keep you from falling asleep or sleeping soundly through the night.

Some people have pet remedies to help them fall asleep. They range from avoiding all muscular activity for the last hour or two just before retiring to the reading of poetry, drinking warm milk, taking a warm bath or assuming certain positions in bed. The value of each remedy lies not in itself but in its induced bromidic effect or in the sense of importance attached to it.

Sleep is nature's way of providing rest for a tired body and a weary mind. Yet it has been proven that the mind retains its re- tentive abilities to absorb outside impressions and in many cases is even more sensitized to them than when fully awake. This ability to receive and to retain impressions has given rise to a new method of teaching and learning while asleep.

Sleep also provides rest for tired muscles but unless we learn to relax them before we fall asleep we will awaken more tired and muscle-weary than before going to bed. Sleep is restful only when we let go of tension, of care, of worry, of anger or of uneasiness.

We are never completely unconscious while asleep, and our body continues to adjust itself to its environment. If we feel cold we snuggle up under the covers; if cramped, we change positions; if warm, we push down or throw off the covers. Studies show that we change positions as often as a few minutes apart and may change them fifty to sixty times during a single night's sleep, without remembering any one of them.

Sleep is the quickest cure for wakeful troubles, the best balm for jangled nerves, the surest restorer of strength and energy. Sleep shuts sorrow's eyes and soothes throbbing pain. It regenerates flagging spirits and grants us the gift of being able to start anew, fresh and clean, every morning.

Form the habit of going to bed at a specific hour night after night. Your body and your nerves will become accustomed to it and habit will help you fall asleep. Learn to shut out disturbing thoughts and relax. And if you still find it hard to go to sleep, follow the advice of the popular song: ". . . Stop counting sheep and start counting your blessings . . ."

Sleep is one form of letting go, of finding repose and release from mental and physical fatigue and nervous tension. Another is muscular relaxation, and Dr. David Fink's ten-week plan of learning how to relax, as elaborated upon in his book, "Release from Nervous Tension", is sound and easy to follow.

To paraphrase him: "Select a suitable time when no one would disturb you, undress and stretch out supine on a bed. Place one pillow under your neck so that your head rolls back toward the head of the bed. Spread your legs a little and place pillows under your knees to bring them upward and outward at a slight angle. Move your hands about eight inches away from your body and put pillows under your elbows, with your hands hanging over the end of the pillows.

"You are now in the right physical position to learn how to relax. Start with your jaw. Let it sag and droop to your chin but keep the lips together. Close your eyes and let the lids meet naturally. Now as you breathe in and out in your usual way, utilize the power of habit in following voiced suggestions and say to your arms: "Let go ... let go ... more ... a little more . . ." Continue ordering them to let loose, to slacken, to let go, until they do.

"Soon, your inhalations and exhalations will slow down, your arms will loosen up and relax with every exhalation and a new sensation will invade you. Your muscular tension will be lessened and you will gain a new sense of renewed muscular strength, of increased bodily tone and vitality. Practice the arm relaxation twice a day, thirty minutes each time, for a period of two weeks.

"The second step in your relaxation practices, beginning with the third week, is to relax your chest muscles. Start with relaxing your arms as you have been doing. When you feel they are heavy and your hands grow warm, start talking to your chest muscles. Ignore your inhalations for the time being. Let them be as usual but every time you exhale say to your chest muscles: "Let go ... let go ... more ... a little more . . ." Continue telling them to let go until you feel them loosen up. Keep this up for a week, twice a day, for half-hour periods.

"Start relaxing your back muscles on the fourth week, the leg muscles on the fifth, the back of the neck on the sixth, and the facial muscles on the seventh. In each case start with the arms, for a few minutes, then with the chest muscles and the others in succession.

"For the eighth week relax the muscles of your scalp to relieve nervous headaches. Let go of the muscles of your eyes for the ninth week. Pretend your eyes are so loose that they will fall out if you do not watch them, and soon you will be rid of the feeling of eye strain. For the tenth and the final week learn to relax the muscles of your vocal chords. Practice speaking slowly, softly, in an even, calm voice, enunciating each word, each syllable, without any strain or special emphasis."

And Dr. Fink concludes "... Ten weeks is a short time to learn to acquire a new skill, yet it is long enough to help you combat emotional conflicts, reduce paralyzing inhibitions, improve your general health, and gain a new sense of freedom from strain and nervous tension."

You can learn to relax while sitting or standing, at work, at home or at play. The secret is not in trying or in exerting an effort but in letting go, in loosening or slackening those muscles which are not in use, at the moment.

If you want to relax while sitting, select a straight-backed chair, sit back as far as possible, plant your feet firmly on the floor and let your arms hang loosely at the sides. Now, let your chin drop until it rests on your chest. Begin to breathe deeply, and as you exhale pretend you have weights at the tips of your fingers and tell your arms to let go. Do it for a couple of minutes. Then use the same ordered suggestions for your feet to let go . . . A few minutes spent in this form of progressive relaxation will do much for you.

You can follow the same idea in relaxing while you stand. Anchor your feet to the floor, keeping them about eight inches apart. Start with drooping your jaw, then with each exhalation tell your arms to let go. After a dozen exhalations your shoulders will lose their stiffness and relax. You follow through with loosening your face muscles and finally the muscles of your chest. The whole thing need not take more than five minutes and yet in that short period of time it can bring you a new sense of ease and freedom.

Normal sleep and muscle relaxations are sound ways to reduce nervous tension, to neutralize compulsions and to minimize inner conflicts. Try them. Follow them and they will surely bring you rest, ease and comfort, as you continue climbing on your stairway to success and happiness, only ten space hours away.

The Twenty-first Hour

HOW TO COPE WITH GRIEF

THIS IS your third week in your thirty day endeavor to reduce your fears, to eliminate harmful habits, to gain self-understanding, to revitalize your mental outlook and learn how to control your feelings and emotions.

If you followed through on the original premise that you are climbing a series of steps on an imaginary stairway, and each stair is another step upward, you have gone up twenty-one steps, you have traveled twenty-one hours in time and space, since you first started and are now only one-quarter of the way from your goal.

You reached the first landing on the seventh day and the second one on the fifteenth. This is your third landing. It is larger, roomier, and has its own protective banister. It gives you greater self-assurance and a new sense of accomplishment. You can tell it in your new awareness that there is more to you and in you than you ever thought it possible. You can tell it in your readiness to go on striving, climbing, learning and improving yourself. You can tell it in your knowledge of how to deal with minor problems, how to reduce frustrations, how to lessen nervous tension and how to gain a greater measure of satisfaction and happiness within the limitations of your age, your economic status and your environment.

Thus, in a sense, you can say that you left your old, drab, dreary "self behind, or below, and can continue your upward climb with mounting self-confidence and assurance. And so, with eyes turned upwards keep on reaching for better, fuller and happier days, as you meet life's problems, sorrows and sudden jolts.

For, somewhere along the line, one of these days, someone near and dear to you may be suddenly taken from you and thus plunge you into the icy folds of grief. The sudden death may prostrate you with sorrow, numb you with dejection and sadden you with bereavement. And, in the midst of your deep loss and despair, you may feel that life is gone for you too, and that nothing will ever heal your sorrowing heart or bring you any consolation.

If you suffered such loss recently do not fight or suppress your pent-up feelings. Do not be ashamed of your emotions. Give way to them. Let the sorrow and the heartache and the inner numbness hold you in their grip and make you cry. Let your grief keep the image of the departed one fully before you. Let your mind and your heart dwell upon your great loss and find expression in tears, in cries, in doleful sighs and mournful lamentations.

Let your tears flow copiously. They are one of nature's safety valves. They stem from the inner recesses of your being and relieve pent-up emotion.

Tears are the great levelers. In the midst of them, the rich and the poor, the mighty and the lowly, the young and the old, have a common bond. All seek and want relief and surcease. All respond to someone else's expression of love, sympathy, compassion, friendship and understanding.

And, if your bereavement came recently, encourage those who come to visit you and comfort you to talk freely about the departed one. Let them dwell upon the great loss, upon the sudden passing of the one you loved and cherished. Let them recall his good deeds, his noble nature, his untimely death, and let them join you in tears and commiseration.

All of these overt expressions are safety valves. They serve to siphon off, little by little, the deep sorrow, the untenable grief, the numbing despair, the feeling of utter futility. In time, they become some of the means by which you rebuild your life upon the ruins of the old, happy, satisfying, commingled existence. They help you to adjust yourself to the changed conditions where you have to go on without the help, support, love or encouragement of the one you lost; when you take up once again the normal cares, needs and duties of your every-day life.

If your loss happened some time ago but you are still grieving too deeply, are still unable to reconcile yourself to your loss and are still incapable of resuming the normal relationships of your daily life you would be wise to consult your priest, rabbi, preacher, minister, doctor or a competent analyst. He would show you how to express your sorrow, how to lessen your pain and how to assuage the inner anguish you bottled up within yourself at the time of your bereavement. He will help you release those pent-up feelings and thus enable you to go on living normally, naturally, without being lost on the way.

You must make peace with the inevitable. You must learn to live with yourself and with others, in spite of your loss. Death is the natural end of all life. The old and the young, the rich and the poor, the simple and the great, all must eventually take that road and "cross the bar" into the great beyond. If you suffered a loss recently you must accept it and bow to the will of God.

Do not close your mind and your heart to life around you. Leave the door open for new contacts, new friends, new concepts and new interests. Leave the door open to those who want to help you rebuild your broken life, who want to be at your side, who want to show you how to find other compensating relationships, which may tend in time to replace, at least in part, the loss you suffered.

Psychiatrists warn us that it is extremely dangerous to repress your grief, to bottle up your sorrows within, to mourn too long and too excessively. It is sure to lead to grave emotional disorders and psychical disturbances. It is normal to grieve and to lament when someone we loved is taken from us, by sickness, accident or natural causes. It is natural to weep, to mourn, to be sorrowful and be saddened by the loss. But, it is imperative for our well-being that we are not swept away by the emotional aftermath.

He who rules our lives and destinies forbids us to grieve too long and lament too bitterly. We must take courage and strength in the realization that God is ever just, ever righteous. We must accept His will and be thankful to Him for having given us the right and the privilege of having had someone we loved and cherished, through the allotted years. We must take heart in the future and our grief must be translated into action, into doing the things the departed one did, in continuing his efforts and aspirations along the same lines, to the best of our abilities.

That should be the normal readjustment after a bereavement. But if you continue to grieve months and months after a death, if your sorrow and despondency linger on, if you remain emotionally unstable and cannot resume normal living, you need psychoanalytical help. Your grief then, is a mask for other disturbances hidden in your unconscious. It could be exaggerated self-pity, a deep feeling of guilt, a play for sympathy, a deeply imbedded hatred, repressed resentments or the unvoiced desire to turn your loss and sorrow into a dependency upon the care and the solicitude of others.

Whatever be the underlying reasons such mental condition is beyond self help or the scope of this book. If you or someone you know has reached that mental block you would do well to seek immediate psychoanalytical help so as to forestall serious mental aberrations. Consult your personal physician at the earliest opportunity and let him make the necessary arrangements.

Many things which touch you deeply for the moment may bring tears to your eyes. Something that you see or hear, a musical passage, a sunrise or a sunset, a dramatic moment in a play or a story, a simple experience, a surge of joy or sadness or any little thing which affects you empathically may bring tears to your eyes. Whatever the case do not be ashamed of your tears. They are not a sign of weakness, of effeminacy or of maudlin sentimentality.

Let your tears come. Let them reveal your inner sensitivity, your close kinship to all men with feeling, sympathy and compassion. Let them show the depth of your response and your evident appreciation of what is glorious, moving, touching, uplifting or appealing to you.

Tears are a form of release, for even in the midst of our deepest sorrow and most tragic moments the tears we shed bring a measure of relief. They become the transition between untenable grief and acceptable sorrow.

The tears of regret, of gratitude and of nostalgia are also a form of release. They often lead to a deeper appreciation of what we have and a greater thankfulness to Him who makes all life possible, tenable and beautiful. The tears of sympathy bring mankind closer together and carry off bitterness and misunderstanding.

The tears of joy are also basically tears of relief as well as tears of recollection. They symbolize the transition from bad to better times, from a worrisome to a carefree, joyful situation. For, in the light of the new day filled with gratitude and thankfulness the tears we shed commingle the memory of the sad times with the release from past tensions and with the freedom and joys yet to come.

When trouble or disaster come unexpectedly upon us or when deep sorrow strikes suddenly many of us go into a state of shock. Adrenalin is pumped freely into the blood stream and the blood pressure rises. The heart speeds up and the digestive system is disturbed. The skin grows cold and the nerves tighten up. We grow tense and some of us "freeze". This is one of the times when nature calls upon one of its safety valves, the flow of tears, to provide an outlet for the pent-up feelings. And, if we deny the natural access to such relief we encourage various physical, mental and emotional disturbances.

So—do not stifle your tears or repress your inner urge to cry, whenever the situation arises. Whether they be tears of joy or sadness, of what was or might have been, of what is or could be, of delight or gratitude, of regret or happiness, of something you see or hear, let the tears come. They express the need for, and provide the means to wash away trouble and tension. They release dammed-up feeling, relieve anger or pain, allay fears or regrets, express thanks or gratitude, or gain needed sympathy and affection.

Tears often relieve a heavy-laden heart and soothe wounds which words or even medication cannot heal. Heart-felt tears shed copiously are the true expression of deep, intense feeling and are akin to prayer. For, like prayer they bring solace, hope and courage, faith and strength and the will to go on trying, striving for and achieving ease of mind.

Aaron Hill said: "Hide not thy tears; weep boldly, and be proud to give the flowing virtue manly ways; it is nature's mark to know an honest heart by . . ." And in the words of Washington Irving: "There is a sacredness in tears. They are not the mark of weakness but of power. They speak more eloquently than ten thousand tongues."

All of this does not imply that you should turn into a "cry-baby" and shed tears at the slightest provocation, but that you evaluate tears in their relation and their expression of true inner feeling and let them serve their natural purpose, as an outlet and release of your emotions.

Let your tears help you to cope with your grief in a bereavement. They are helpful in alleviating part of the sorrow. But what are some of the other ways you can use to meet your grief and compensate, in part, for your loss? Supposing you were to ask this question of yourself: "If I were suddenly taken from those who love me what are the steps I would like them to take, what are the things I would want them to go on doing, after I am gone . . . ?"

You might have a whole list of such items or activities. Follow the same trend of thought and ask yourself: "What were the aims, the wishes or the desires of the departed one? How could I continue the same projects or interests? Would he prefer me to go on crying, grieving, lamenting, and do nothing else or would he rather see me 'buckle down' to carrying on his work? What would be the best way to follow in his steps . . . ?"

Find the proper answers to these and similar questions and put them into immediate operation. Then, before you realize it your feeling of futility will begin to dwindle and gradually disappear. You will suddenly feel at greater ease, because you would be doing what he or she wanted you to do. You would be perpetuating the aims and the efforts, the hopes and the aspirations of the departed one, and in the depth of your being feel closer and nearer to him.

And as time passes you will have gained new strength and courage and hope as you learn how to bear up the best you can under trials, adversities, grief and tribulations. Time and work are the great healers of sorrow and strife. Put them to good use and let them help you find ease and comfort, joy and consolation, as you go on working, striving, living your life.

The Twenty-second Hour

HOW TO BENEFIT BY DISCONTENT

DISCONTENT is an emotional feeling. The dictionary defines it as restlessness, displeasure or disappointment and gives "dissatisfaction" as a synonym, making the two words interchangeable.

But to the psychoanalyst, the term "discontent" has a deeper and more significant meaning than dissatisfaction. The latter has reference to being displeased or dissatisfied, the first to the unwillingness to be pleased. This implies a conscious rejection of acceptance, a definite volition not to take a given condition or situation submissively or complacently.

Dissatisfaction, in its generic sense, is part of life. We are never completely satisfied with what we are, with what we do, with what we have and with what the future holds for us. We always want something more, something else or something better.

But the degree of dissatisfaction is not the same in all cases. In some instances it is only a grumble or wish-thinking. How often have you heard it expressed something like this: "If I had been given the chance others got ... If only I had the same "breaks". ... If I had the parents, the influential in-laws, the "push" or the good fortune that fell into so-and-so's lap ... If my parents had given me the start ... If I had been in a position to grab opportunity as so-and-so did ... If I were twenty years younger ... If I were free to go or to start anew ... If I had his or her looks ... If I were willing to sell my soul . . . But . . ."

And the complainant "goes off on another tack", enumerating all the mishaps and misfortunes that befell him and all the reasons why he never got ahead. But if the truth were known, his alibis and excuses are "sour grapes", because had his dissatisfaction been strong enough and had he backed it by real desire and incentive he would have never remained placid and complaisant. He would have never accepted conditions as they were. He would have tried to do something about them rather than voice his dissatisfaction with lip service.

The true, sincere desire cannot be stilled by words or promises, and the wish-thinker fools only himself. He will always have the "breaks" against him. His right time or proper time will never come, and should opportunity ever knock at his door he will be too busy bemoaning his bad luck to hear the knock.

Dissatisfaction is usually passive, discontent is active. Dissatisfaction can be only discomfort, uneasiness or disappointment, discontent has a deeper sense of disquietude and in most cases is backed by the urge to do something about the situation.

If you are dissatisfied with your job there may be one or more reasons for it. Among them could be the type of work you do, the time spent at it, your co-workers or superiors, the pay you receive, the limited opportunities for advancement, your attitude toward your duties and responsibilities or your lack of interest, application, vision and initiative.

Your dissatisfaction may lead to disinterest, to resentments, to open antagonisms and to deliberate disregard of company rules and regulations. It may also lead to inner conflicts and frustrations. You dislike your job and everything connected with it but you dare not or cannot give up the money you earn. Thus, you are stymied and the inner conflicts grow and grow.

If you are dissatisfied with your family set-up, the reasons may be in the way you live, in your neighborhood, in your family habits or conduct, in your lack of interest or cooperation, or in your mental attitude. If the dissatisfactions within you stem from the friends you have or the company you keep, the reasons may be in the fact that they are not your kind, too rich for your blood or too set in their ways.' They may be drinking too much or playing too hard or living too high and there is no common bond between you.

If your dissatisfaction comes from what you are or what you are not, from the seemingly dismal prospects ahead, then perhaps you ought to start taking stock of your abilities, make a fresh start and reroute yourself. It may be hard for a while to begin anew but waiting will not make it any easier. So—decide now to go ahead, because time will be in your favor, and the efforts you exert will make you strong.

Turn your dissatisfaction into creative, directive discontent. Nothing has ever been accomplished by waiting, by hoping, by wishing or just drifting along. Man's discontent has ever been his motivating power to try, to seek and to strive for something better. Without it man would have never gone beyond the cave and stone age. Without it you and I would not be enjoying the ease, the comfort, the developments and the discoveries of our age.

Avoid sameness and lack of interest in what you do. They breed boredom, build up fatigue, foster exhaustion, destroy initiative and stifle alertness. These, in turn, awaken resentments, arouse frustrations, nurture animosities and promote inner conflicts.

The simple solution for sustaining vocational interest would be to do only what we want to do or what we enjoy doing, or perhaps do nothing at all, but these are hardly feasible for someone in moderate circumstances, who has to work so as to live.

The next solution would be to inject an element of play or surprise, of a contest or a competition, of study or an induced interest in the task before you. This may sound difficult but it is not so, if you learn to apply a little thought, pretense, illusion, ingenuity or imagination to the job or the chore before you.

Of course, if you violently dislike your present job and find every moment at it a new source of physical and mental torment, quit as soon as you can or else you will go to pieces. If, however, the job holds good possibilities and your dissatisfaction stems from a mental attitude, here are several ways to deal with it:

1st. Fire yourself today, as of this hour, and imagine yourself applying for the same job tomorrow morning. Visualize yourself as a stranger, as a newcomer to the city, as someone who would like to get into that field and with that company and build his future around it. As such, you will evaluate the advantages and the opportunities ahead and you would try to convince your future employer that you are the right man for the job.

This mental reevaluation of your present connections may prove to be a revelation to you. It may give you a new slant on things. It may show you where you fall short of the company's expectations, where you are missing the boat, where you fail to take advantage of the existing opportunities for your advancement. It may change your mental attitude and give you the "push", the impetus you need to do better and be in line for promotion.

2nd. See your job and its duties as a direct challenge to your ability, intelligence and resourcefulness. Try to find ways to do the same things you do a little quicker, easier or better than before. Visualize your job as your employer does, in the light of what he needs, wants or expects to have. All of this may lead you to uncover short-cuts, savings, improvements, and thereby bring you due rewards in money and advancement.

3rd. Think of your job in the terms of a problem in motion, and of the results as a study in effects. Pretend that you are a student, a research specialist, an efficiency expert, an advisor or counselor. Look for ways to speed up production, to cut costs, to eliminate motions, to improve the looks or the quality, to add a touch of something new and different to the mode of operation. It is surprising how often such creative thought brings highly desirable and remunerative results and leads to promotion.

4th. Evaluate your tasks, your services or the product in the light of modern needs and possible changes. What was good for your father has little use for you today and none, whatsoever, to the next generation. Try to visualize the job, the service or the product in use in other fields and under totally different conditions or circumstances. This may lead you to discover new ways, new methods or new processes of how to make the product or the service more useful, more desirable, more valuable or more salable and, in turn, bring you welcomed returns in money and position.

5th. Make a study of your field of activity. Trace the job, the service or the product to its beginning. Learn where or how it started, what changes took place throughout the years and how it reached its present uses or values. This may start you on many interesting ramifications in research and comparison. It is bound to add color, beauty, interest and even pleasure to what you are doing. It may carry you far afield, broaden your concepts, increase your knowledge, add to your importance and prepare you for the higher job ahead with corresponding increases in pay, in prestige and importance. It may even establish you as an authority in the field and lead to national recognition.

No job, no matter how ordinary it may appear, is entirely devoid of interest, of accomplishment, of personal gratification. It is a matter of mental attitude, and your discontent may often be a blessing in disguise. It may lead you to see changes or improvements. It may prompt you to seek new outlets for expression and that leads to improvement.

If your discontent stems from family relationships check into the underlying reasons. You may be the "fly in the ointment", the disturbing or the contributing factor. You may be the one who needs to change his attitude, his mode of behavior.

If your discontent comes from the friends you have and the company you keep you might do well to drop them. This is not as difficult as it appears. Begin by missing meetings or contacts with those whom you wish to avoid. Try not to frequent the same spots or if you have to go there change or shorten the hours. Plan your leisure-time activities along different lines and in different ways. Try to make new contacts, acquire new skills, join new groups, make new friends, and before long your old haunts and activities will be left behind.

If your discontent comes from the realization that you are not getting anywhere, that you are in a rut and must get out of it, then by all means get out and make a fresh start.

Begin anew. Evaluate your abilities and tendencies, decide upon what you know you can do best and strike out fresh and clean. You may meet many obstacles, hardships, setbacks and disappointments. But you will be doing what you wanted to do. That in itself will strengthen you and help you utilize your hidden reserves of stamina and determination.

Believe in yourself. Believe in your abilities and capacities. Respect your inner urges and your desire to do what you like to do. Back it with all the will power you can command. Build up the right attitude toward what you are doing and trying to accomplish.

That will place the power of habit and purpose behind your efforts and by the same token add meaning and value to your life.

Your discontent can be your closest ally. Direct it into the proper channels and you will reap its benefits.

HOW TO LIVE WITH YOURSELF

FROM DAYS IMMEMORIAL our teachers, philosophers and spiritual leaders have been counseling us to know ourselves.

What is meant by it? Simply this, you are the mirror which reflects your little world and the world around you. By knowing and understanding your own urges and impulses and by evaluating what you like or dislike, want or appreciate, need or desire, you can tell what others are looking for and thus be in a better position to adapt yourself and live happier among them.

Trust and listen to the inner promptings of your heart. Emerson put it in these words: "What is true to you in the privacy of your own heart is true to all men . . ." And Shakespeare said: ". . . To thine own self be true, and it must follow, as the night the day, thou canst not then be false to any man . . ."

Yet most of us have never taken this counsel to heart or given much thought to its uses and benefits. We stumble blithely on and do not know how to live with ourselves or with others. Many of us have never learned how to be self-reliant or self-sufficient and thus enjoy our own company. As a result, loneliness and unhappiness "dog" our footsteps and "stalk" our ways.

If this happens to be the case with you, it may be due to one of these reasons:

1. A lack of common interests with other people. You may be confining yourself, either by choice or by accident, to narrow fields

of activity and are unwilling to widen them. You may be too set in your ways, too arbitrary in your preferences or inclinations or too adamant in your views and opinions. You look only for those who have similar tastes and when you fail to find them travel on alone, in misery and loneliness.

2. An inability to mix easily and readily with others. Perhaps you expect too much and refuse to make allowances for differences in views, interests and inclinations. For instance, do you disap prove of small talk or card-playing and are quick to voice your dis pleasure? Do you make believe that you are above such silly ways of spending time? Do you assume superior airs and expect people to cater to you? Do you usually refuse to participate in any activity which does not come up to your high (?) standards? If so, you are hardly welcomed by any group and therefore find yourself alone and miserable most of the time.

3. An inability to be among people, and get along with them. You may be too eager or effusive or may lean to the other extreme and be too furtive or fearful. In the first instance you overwhelm people with your anxiety to please, with your readiness to serve, with your willingness to give of yourself. In the second instance you hold yourself apart, shy clear of direct participation in various activities and are reluctant to do or say anything which might involve you in any way. In either case, you put others on the de fensive and arouse their suspicions or apprehensions. This affects your normal relations or contacts with others and promotes lone liness.

4. A demand for attention or interest. You may be looking for continual sympathy or commiseration, for respect or attention. You try to use people as your receptacles in which to empty your woes, sorrows, complaints and disappointments, and feel hurt or displeased when they fail to sit by and listen to you. You open your heart to anyone who is nearby and put him under the obliga tion of being your confidant, the unwilling bearer of your burdens. Most people do not relish it. They show their displeasure by being disinterested, by discouraging your confidences or by trying to avoid being near you. Thus, you find yourself alone.

5. A nervous or high-strung temperament. You may be a nervous

or high-strung individual, by nature or by habit. You cannot sit still for a moment or relax for any length of time. You have to be doing something or going places all the time. This tends to make people around you fidgety and ill-at-ease. Soon they begin to shun your company and thus you find yourself alone most of the time.

6. A tendency to gossip or to criticize. You may have acquired the habit of talking freely about people, of passing out comments and observations. This may be innocent in itself, with no intent to harm or belittle anyone. Yet, it carries many implications. Your remarks may be changed or colored in the process of repeating and awaken needless hostilities. Or, you may be a consistent "kibitzer", a criticizer, a belittler, a fault-finder. Whatever the case, such practices seldom endear you to anyone. They do not build friendships, do not promote good will or good feeling and only add to your loneliness or unhappiness.

Learn to live with yourself before you undertake to live amiably with others, but do not get all wrapped up in yourself. Learn to benefit by the value of solitude, where you can get away from people at times, when you can commune with yourself and enjoy the company of your own thoughts.

Our sages, teachers, writers and spiritual leaders have been urging us, through the years, to look inwardly, to withdraw into ourselves from time to time, to build a sanctuary within our minds and heart, where we can retire occasionally and through such deliberate seclusion look for ways of self-exploration and self-evaluation.

You can be your own worst enemy or your greatest friend. It is in how you behave, in how you use your good and bad qualities, in how you ignore or utilize your potentialities, in how you follow or disregard the dictates of your heart. How well the Bard of Avon put it: "Go to your bosom, knock there and ask your heart what doth it know . . ." Add one more line to complete his basic thought, " . . . and listen to what your heart doth say . . ."

Of course, it is difficult to make appraisals of ourselves, and do it impartially, objectively. We are prone to amplify or magnify the failures of others and justify or nullify our own shortcomings. Yet, by cultivating the calming, quieting, relaxing effects of true solitude we can begin to see ourselves as others do and thereby reach self-understanding.

Some people confuse loneliness with solitude, as interchangeable terms, but the two have nothing in common. Loneliness is an aloneness which we dislike and try to avoid, even at the cost of our self-respect; solitude is the expressed desire to be alone, a desire deliberately sought, encouraged or cultivated. Loneliness is a feeling of depression because one is alone and companionless; solitude is the voluntary withdrawal from contact with others, into the completeness of personal thought. Loneliness is often the unvoiced dependence upon the presence of others to offset an inner emptiness; solitude is the purposeful retreat into reflection, the communion with one's inner thoughts and directed contemplations.

You are the least alone when in the midst of solitude^ No companion can be as close, as unobtrusive and yet as helpful in promoting creative thought, and that, in turn, is the road to progress and to achievement.

Solitude can be as refreshing to the mind and to the spirit as restful sleep is to the body. It leads to calm meditation, soothes troubled nerves, fosters serenity, relieves nervous tension, induces repose and engenders relaxation in the midst of tumult and confusion.

Meditation, as practiced by the Hindu mystics and the followers of Pantheism, is not day-dreaming or mental meandering. It is a directive thought control through a deliberate withdrawal from one's immediate surroundings. It is a purposeful retirement to an inner state of contemplation, a deliberate concentration upon a set trend of thought, fully and steadily maintained for the desired period of time, against all interference or interruption.

Learn to enjoy your own company by drawing upon your own knowledge, memory, experiences or resources. Learn to be self-sufficient, and you will gain the much-desired sense of personal independence. Perhaps that is what Ralph Waldo Emerson had in mind when he wrote: "It is easy in the world to live after the world's opinion; it is easy in solitude to live after our own. But the great man is he who in the midst of the crowd keeps with perfect sweetness the independence of his solitude."

Solitude teaches you to appreciate your own company and be less demanding of others. It shows you how to make peace with yourself, with things and conditions beyond your control. It keeps you from getting onto a pedestal of self-assumed righteousness or indignation and judge people on the basis of your preconceived notions, ideas, beliefs or convictions. It brings home to you the realization that to live with others amiably, happily, you must make allowances for differences in views and opinions, so that they, in turn, will be willing to listen to and show respect for your likes, views and contentions.

Philip James Bailey had that in mind when he wrote: "We live in deeds . . . in thoughts . . . in feelings. We should count time by heart-throbs . . . He most lives who thinks most, feels the noblest, sets the best . . ."

These are the ways in which you can learn to live with yourself in the midst of trouble and confusion. Follow some of these suggestions and then it will be easier for you to fill your mind with pleasant, peaceful, cheerful, uplifting thoughts and thus cultivate the proper frame of mind.

Follow these ideas and they will add color, beauty, joy and happiness to your daily life.

The Twenty-fourth Hour

HOW TO COMBAT LONELINESS

NEARLY EVERYONE has come under the ravages of loneliness at one time or another. It is like a disease. It breeds boredom, discontent, discouragement, misery and can make us sick. There are no medical treatments for it because it is an induced or an acquired state of mind and only your own efforts in changing your mental attitude can help you to combat your loneliness.

Loneliness and aloneness, although commonly considered synonymous, are not the same. Aloneness has reference to being isolated or separated from people by choice or circumstance; loneliness is a need, a craving for contact or association with others. Aloneness is the state of being alone or segregated but it does not imply that such person is forlorn, forgotten, miserable or unhappy; loneliness is lowness of spirit, a feeling of depression, a sense of dejection, the lack of love, sympathy, friends and companionship.

If you are lonely it may be due to one or more of these contributory factors:

1st. Your loneliness may be due to your line of work. If your eyes are glued to the eyes of a telescope all the time, if you are a miner or a prospector or a keeper of a lighthouse, to mention only four categories of work, your occupation forces you to be a lone, solitary worker. Hence, you must learn to live with yourself within the limits of your secluded occupation and enjoy your own company or else look for something else.

2nd. Your loneliness may be due to a deep inner unhappiness, brought about by grief, sorrow or anguish. You are so upset emotionally, so entrenched in your miseries, that no one can reach you. You feel lonely and depressed and terribly alone even in the midst of your closest friends and relatives. Such condition is, fortunately, temporary and eventually wears off.

3rd. Your loneliness may be due to a self-centered attitude, aided, fostered and abetted by a selfish nature. It tends to sensitize you to trivial discomforts or hurts and brings needless misery and unhappiness. Psychologists say that such form of loneliness is often a mask for self-pity, for the craving of care and attention. You feel sorry for yourself and you build up a series of false beliefs and premises, that you are not wanted or needed or appreciated, that friends and strangers alike want to hurt you. You luxuriate in your self-inflicted hurts and find consolation and gratification in your apparent misery and loneliness.

4th. Your loneliness may be due to assumptions. For instance, a close friend of yours passed you on the street or elsewhere and failed to greet you or pay attention to you. You assume it was deliberate and grow incensed. Your ego or pride or self-esteem was affected and as your surmises grow your chagrin and resentment grow. You hasten to accuse, to censure or to condemn. Perhaps the person involved was completely innocent of the so-called slight or insult to you. He may have been in a hurry and had no time to stop and visit with you or he may have been too absorbed in his immediate problem to notice you. But you are beyond simple explanations. Your accusations, in a distorted form, finally reach the one who had supposedly insulted you and strikes back. The misunderstanding grows. Before long you reap the harvest of alienation and that starts you on the road to loneliness.

5th. Your loneliness may be due to habitual mistrust. You consider yourself a very important person, especially if you have a little of the worldly goods, and take it for granted that people have you on their minds, or are looking for ways to "milk" you. So, you keep aloof and play "cagey" and show it very plainly. People resent it and before long begin to shun you.

6th. Your loneliness may be due to a real or an assumed lack of self-reliance. You appear or make-believe that you are so help less, so dependent upon the goodness and the kindness of others that people have to cater to you or be beholden to you. They resent the attendant responsibilities or obligations and try to avoid your company.

If one or more of these conditions contribute to your loneliness and tend to make you miserable and unhappy, you can combat them in one of these ways:

1. Stop looking for a "red carpet" or expecting special con siderations when someone invites you to a party, a meeting or a gathering.

2. Stop "putting up your nose in the air", showing your disdain or voicing your disapproval if the group you are with or the activ ity which interests them is not to your liking.

3. Stop wearing your heart on your sleeve, burdening friends and strangers alike with your real or fancied troubles and expect ing their continual sympathy or commiseration.

4. Stop judging people too hastily, jumping to conclusions or making unwarranted assumptions, without allowing for differences in opinion or considering conditions and circumstances.

5. Stop imagining that people are always talking about you or are forever scheming to slight you or belittle you. You are not that important to anyone.

6. Stop being officious in your attitudes, dictatorial in your manner or arbitrary in your decisions. That is hardly the way to gain friends and influence people.

7. Stop making snide remarks, being sarcastic or belittling people just because you do not like them or because they fail to please you for the moment.

8. Start giving of yourself freely, readily, without asking for or expecting immediate returns for your help, your favors or gratuities.

9. Start showing an interest and taking an active part in what ever others are doing for the moment, especially if you are one of the group, even if you have to pretend for the time being.

10. Start offering your help, services or cooperation even when you and the others know you cannot do much. Be natural about it and let it not be in the form of a grand gesture or a bid for applause.

11. Start looking for ways to repay favors as soon as you can. Learn to be sociable, amenable, hospitable and be quick to show your appreciation and express your thankfulness.

12. Start overlooking minor discrepancies, a slip of the tongue or an occasional faux pas, when you are with others. And, even when such things annoy you or irritate you, pass over them lightly and as unobtrusively as possible, without calling anyone's atten tion to it or offending the person involved.

13. Start getting into the spirit of things when you are part of a group, even if you have to play-act all of the time, so as not to dampen the occasion and spoil the fun or the pleasure of any of the others.

14. Start making your peace with people, with things and con ditions, especially if there is nothing you can do to change them or eliminate them.

15. Start looking for oneness with your spiritual self. Build up your inner reserves of sufficiency and independence and cultivate an abiding faith in Him, who is your Creator and Preserver.

These are the ways to combat loneliness in connection with

other people, but there are also other ways by learning to be your own company, by utilizing your personal, private resources.

Your loneliness can be minimized and dissipated by cultivating the mental attitude of being satisfied with what you have and not grabbing at, grasping or grappling for more and more of worldly goods. It is in being thankful to God for your health, for your family, your friends and all the things you can enjoy today, now.

It is in your awareness that you can store and accumulate, at will, beautiful memories, pleasant moments, happy incidents, inspiring thoughts, cheerful remembrances and then be able to recall them, whenever you wish, in all of their enjoyable details. It is in your having patience with yourself and the people around you and not being vexed, troubled or irritated by trivial discomforts or annoyances.

All of these desirable things are a frame of mind, called contentment, and you can cultivate it in the privacy of your home and in the depths of your heart and mind.

Perhaps that is what Robert Greene had in mind when he wrote:

Sweet are the thoughts that savor of content;
The quiet mind is richer than a crown.
Sweet are the nights in careless slumber spent;
The poor estate scorns fortune's angry frown.
Such sweet content, such minds, such sleep, such bliss,
Beggars enjoy, and princes oft do miss.

Contentment and satisfaction and freedom from loneliness go hand in hand. They are the faithful, grateful, fruitful use of what we have, of what we think and what we accept. This prompted Sir Edward Dwyer to write:

My *mind to me a kingdom is;*
Such perfect joy therein I find,
As far excels all earthly bliss
That God of Nature has assigned.
Though much I want that most would have

Yet still my mind forbids to crave.
Some have too much, yet still do crave;
I little have and seek no more.
They are but poor though much they have,
And I am rich with little store.
They poor, I rich; they beg, I give;
They lack, 1 leave; they pine, I live.
Content I live; this is my stay,—
I seek no more than may suffice.
I press to bear no haughty sway;
Look, what I lack my mind supplies.
Lo, thus I triumph like a king,
Content with what my mind doth bring.
I laugh not at another's loss;
I grudge not another's gain.
No worldly wave my mind can toss;
I brook what is another's bane.
I fear no foe, nor fawn on friend;
I loathe not life, nor dread my end.
My wealth is health and perfect ease;
My conscience clear my chief defense.
I never seek by bribes to please
Nor by desert to give offense.
Thus do I live, thus will I die;
Would all did so as well as I.

What beautiful, peace-promoting thoughts! What good they can do you, in combating your loneliness, in promoting your satisfaction and contentment, as you continue climbing higher and higher on your private stairway to success and happiness, only 6 space hours away.

The Twenty-fifth Hour

HOW TO MAKE TIME YOUR FRIEND

IN ITS INEXORABLE FLIGHT into infinity time is ever on the move and yet, in our mind's eye, it has the facility to rush head on or to stop and remain immobile for a while, untouched by what is, what has been or what may come.

Time sweeps on and on, impervious to change, unmindful of what transpires, but it touches us and affects us at every foot of its journey. Nothing that happens is ever lost, for whatever it be it leaves its indelible marks upon the pages of time and remains imprisoned therein. Astronomers tell us that many galaxies of stars we see today are hundreds of light years away and are recording for us, at this moment, what happened there hundreds and thousands of years ago.

Time as we measure it and evaluate it, aside from its relation to space, to motion and to perspective, has three levels which we term the past, the future and the present. Each has its handmaidens and each is within your reach and within your ability to manipulate to some extent, even though your span of life is but a speck of dust in the mighty whirlwinds of the cosmos.

Memory is the handmaiden of what has been, the record of our past. Every feeling, emotion, sensation or experience we ever had is recorded somewhere in the voluminous catalogs of our conscious or unconscious memory and can be recalled with or without direct volition.

In the light of memory time has no meaning. The days or the years which separate us from a given feeling or experience are no barrier to memory for it spans all chasms of time or space and reaches what it wishes to recall in split seconds. Memory can separate or combine, select or delete, transpose or superimpose one remembrance upon another in a fantastic fashion, by accident or by design, without any regard to actual sequences or consequences.

What is more, memory can color, filter, simplify, modify, amplify or magnify the mode, the manner, the sequence, the value or the importance of various incidents from one time to the next, in complete reversals of former recalls so as to justify or satisfy the wish, the need or the circumstance.

Memory also has the facility to take you back into a past beyond the normal areas of awareness. Theosophists believe in former existences and claim that the strange, mystifying sudden flashes of odd memories which reach you from time to time are the snatches of true reminiscences or experiences of former existences.

Dreams and visions are the handmaidens of the future, indications of what is to come. Some of us have extrasensory perceptions and are said to be able to foresee or foretell the future. Others depend upon forebodings, premonitions or so-called intuitions and plan their futures accordingly.

Contemplation, meditation and directive concentration, while dealing with the future, are in reality the handmaidens of the present. They hold time immobile and imprison it in the immediate consciousness for the desired period of time, even though a thousand clocks tick off the passing moments and drop them, one by one, into the bottomless pits of infinity.

In so far as you are concerned, time is the present which you fashioned yesterday and time in your future will be what you m ake of the present. One is closely interlinked with the other and like a paved roadway, built brick by brick and day by day, sets the pace and the distance of your personal route through life.

Make time your friend. Take from the past only those things which you want to keep and let the rest vanish into the limbo of oblivion. Let what you keep become your treasure house of pleasant, beautiful memories to cherish through the years. Let them soften the blows of fate, ease your pain and mellow the cares of today.

Make time your friend. Put into your future your hopes and dreams of better days to come. Imbue it with faith and courage.

Picture it in bright, warm, beautiful colors, without groundless fears and needless apprehensions and without tacking onto it the sorrows of yesterday and the cares of today.

Make the most of the time you have, today. The secret of deriving happiness, contentment and satisfaction lies not in doing only what you like or want to do but in adapting yourself to every situation and in learning how to derive joys and pleasure in what you can do or have to do—now.

Make the most of your time and let it be your friend in these ways:

1st. Take more time to think and to consider all the consequences before you say or do something in a rash, angry, spiteful or vindictive mood. Feeling, sentiment, emotion and impetuosity have their place and value but when allowed to go unchecked or rule you without restraint are sure to bring you needless pain, worry, trouble, disappointment and estrangements.

2nd. Take more time to laugh. No matter how serious a given situation might be it has its lighter and humorous side. Learn to laugh easily, readily, naturally, even at yourself, if need be. Laughter has a definite therapeutic value. It promotes deeper diaphragmatic breathing and oxygenates the blood. It is an emotional safety valve and siphons off cares, worries and anxieties.

Laughter eases pain and clears the air of hostility or misunderstanding. It lightens chores, dissipates fear, soothes a troubled spirit and drives off despondency. It promotes a sense of humor, brightens your days, cheers those around you and helps you to make and keep friends.

3rd. Take more time to dream. Let your fancies roam and let them echo the secret wishes of your heart. If you are in business dream of heights to be reached and use your creative and imaginative powers to attain those heights. Whatever be your tasks or your interests dreaming about them being better, nicer and more enjoyable is sure to bring its eventual rewards. We are such stuff as dreams are made of and you can encourage those dreams which bring you joy, cheer, gladness and satisfaction. Many a dream of yesterday is a reality today because someone dared to dream . . .

4th. Take more time to play. Play is as important to your physical and mental well-being as food and rest. Whether it be a game or a sport, an indoor or an outdoor activity, a simple pastime or an important absorbing hobby, give it the time and the attention you can spare and let it add to your joys of living.

5th. Take more time to love. Without love life has no value, no beauty, no meaning. Love is as old as time and yet it is ever new, ever young, ever interesting, for like time itself it goes on and on. You are never too old, too poor, too lowly or too humble to love and be loved. Cultivate the fruits of love tenderly, steadily, and they will multiply your joys of living a thousandfold.

6th. Take more time to build friendships. You can do it anywhere at any time and you do not have to be rich, handsome, powerful or influential to make friends. Friendship is not dependent upon and is not affected by those things. It is not who you are but what you are that counts. Friendship is the open door to trust, to kindness, to loyalty, regard, confidence and devotion. Treat the friends you make as you would want them to treat you and follow this old maxim: "Write the faults of your friends upon the moving sands of time but etch their virtues upon the tablets of love and memory."

7th. Take more time to do the things you wanted to do or feel that you ought to do but for some reason have been putting them off. Make the start now. Put time to work for you—now. Do not delay any longer. You may never again have as good an opportunity.

8th. Take more time to eat not for the purpose of consuming more food but to eat less hurriedly and masticate every bite. Give your salivary glands and the ptyalin the time needed to convert starches into dextrose before they enter your stomach. Your twenty-six feet of rolled, turned and twisted intestines have enough work to do without being forced to accept dry, hard, half-chewed chunks of miscellaneous food which has had no chance to be dexterized and pepsin-ized to aid the digestive processes.

Linger longer at your meals whether at home or elsewhere. Make it an ironclad rule never to bring any of your cares, problems, worries, quarrels, censures or disagreements to the dinner table. Make mealtime a slow-eating, well-masticating, pleasure-building time and then whatever you eat will "stay put" with you. It will never give you heartburn, indigestion or other digestive disturbances.

9th. Take more time to relax even if it be only for a few minutes. Do it by changing pace in whatever you are doing, either by slowing down, speeding up or stopping altogether. Do it, by taking a "break," even if it is only to take a drink, walk across the room or exchange casual remarks with someone else. Do it, by relaxing, wherever you happen to be, and whether you are sitting or standing.

The secret of relaxing lies not in trying or in exerting the effort but in letting the tense muscles go limp and loose. If you are sitting and want to relax tense neck muscles, do it in this way. Straighten in your seat and push your spine back against the chair as much as you can. Anchor your feet firmly to the floor and let your arms hang loosely from the shoulders. Bring your chin down to rest on your chest. Now imagine that your head is mounted on a sensitized swivel joint and begin to rotate it from right to left in a full circular motion, describing as large a circle as you can. Keep the neck loose and slack and let your head roll as if it were to fall off at any moment. After a dozen or more rotations from right to left change to a left-to-right movement. Continue this exercise for two minutes and you will have a new sense of ease and freedom, and the tenseness of your neck muscles will be gone completely.

To relax tired arms, begin to breathe slowly and with each exhalation let go of your arm muscles. Make believe that there is a heavy weight at the tip of each finger and let your arms sag. Continue doing it until your shoulders loosen and your hands begin to feel warm, and soon the muscle tension of your arms will disappear. Follow the same procedure with your leg muscles, with the chest, with your facial muscles and before long you will be enjoying the benefits of relaxation.

10th. Take more time to pray. Prayer promotes inner peace and serenity. Prayer is the conscious effort to reach God, the source of eternal life, the fountainhead of love and mercy. The mere effort to commune with the Almighty engenders hope and faith and courage and belief. Let prayer be the tie that binds you to nobler thoughts and aspirations, and new joys will be yours.

11th. Take more time to develop an interest in something other than your work or allied activities. Let it broaden your concepts and widen your contacts with others. Join one or more worthwhile groups and take an active part in what they do, and if none suits you start one of your own and become the leader, the organizer, the instigator.

12th. Take more time to give of yourself. The Bible says that he who is interested only in himself is small and petty but he who gives freely, gladly and readily of himself has the whole wide world before him. It takes no special efforts or talents to do it. At times only a ready smile, a kind word, a friendly gesture, a pat on the back, a sign of approval or a word of appreciation is all you need to give of yourself, and to bring joy and happiness to others.

13th. Take more time to enjoy what you have or can enjoy. Stop being envious of others and feeling sorry for yourself. A larger house, a newer car, more gadgets for your home, more clothes in your closet or more money in the bank will not bring you one moment of health or one minute of happiness. You can be as rich as Croesus and yet be the poorest person alive, if you have no peace of mind and no joy or pleasure in your heart.

14th. Take time out to use your sense perceptions and become more appreciative of what you can see, hear, touch, taste, feel or experience. Life and nature in its wondrous forms and manifestations is all around you. The heavens above, the changing seasons, the song of the wind, the patter of rain, the flowers in bloom, the laugh of a child, the voice of a friend, the warm look of someone you love. All of these and more are yours to enjoy if you but take the time for it.

15th. Take more time to nourish your mind. It needs food almost as much as your body, but unfortunately it cannot use hunger pains to remind you of its needs. To ignore your mind and let it wander along aimlessly is to let it vegetate and invite mental sclerosis. Keep your mind supplied with live, positive, cheerful thoughts. Store it with happy incidents and pleasant remembrances. Give it the chance to acquire new interests, broaden your concepts and widen your horizons. Put to better use its retentive qualities and its imaginative facilities. Make it your ready repository of all the things you want to keep and to recall. And, no matter how many calendar years you add to your age your mind will remain active, alert and ever young.

Stop chasing or pursuing time. You cannot possibly catch up with it and any minutes saved at the expense of personal peril or nervous tension are too costly to keep. Stop the needless, foolish, useless hurrying and begin to take life calmer, easier.

Make time your friend. Use it to add to your joys and pleasures of living. Then, and only then, will time be on your side and your life will be brighter and happier.

The Twenty-sixth Hour

HOW TO INCREASE RETIREMENT PLEASURES

ARE YOU A MAN, in good physical and mental condition, who reached your retirement age recently and find it not at all as relaxing and enjoyable as you expected it to be? Have the plans you made and the dreams you dreamed about leisure-time activities gone completely astray? Is there growing friction between you and your wife, your family and your friends? Are you at cross-purposes with yourself and with the world around you?

There are understandable and justifiable reasons for your unhappiness and disappointments. You made drastic changes in your old, firmly established routines and have not adjusted yourself as yet to the new way of life. You have too much time on your hands and do not know what to do with it. You miss your old ties, contacts, duties, associations and mode of daily procedure and have not as yet replaced them with something equally as interesting. You are on edge, irritable, short-tempered, upset, angry, bewildered and unhappy. You want to and you have to strike back and the one who carries the brunt of it is your wife.

She has more cares and responsibilities than ever before, because although *you* retired from active work she has not. In most instances her duties have been increased manyfold. For years past, you left for work at a certain hour every morning and the day was hers to use as desired. She had her chores and routines and was used to them.

But, with your retirement, your wife's old routine went overboard. You are at home morning, noon and night. She has to plan, prepare and serve three or four meals a day. She is no longer a free agent. You are around all the time, free to make comments, to criticize her and to make life harder for her.

So—if you have recently retired from active work, are not as yet settled in your new freedom and want to make the intervening period pleasant and enjoyable for you and your wife, do it in these ways:

1st. Try to maintain your old hours in so far as the morning and the evening meals are concerned.

2nd. Do not hang around the house all day long and get into your wife's way. Find something to do away from home. Go to the movies or visit friends or keep yourself occupied at something elsewhere.

3rd. Do not meddle with or interfere in any way with your wife's home chores. Stay out of the kitchen, no matter how strong your desire to try your hand at cooking or baking.

4th. If your wife happens to snap at you or grows somewhat sharp at times make allowances for it. You are under foot and now and then she may find it awkward and irritable.

5th. If you are planning little trips or other enjoyable things have her in mind. Ask her to join you even when you both know that she cannot participate, for the time being.

6th. Try to make things easier for her. This period in your lives can be one of the happiest. Now supposing that for tomorrow morning you pretended that she was an important guest at your house and were to serve her breakfast in bed. Or, supposing that on the following day you made believe that you were courting her as in the olden days and were to bring her flowers and "date" her for an evening out. Would she like it? Would you enjoy it?

7th. Do not seek to "change her ways" at this stage in your married life. You liked her as she was and let her have her "say" in matters pertaining to the home and to herself. Why start looking for changes or disagreements now?

8th. Stop finding fault with her household chores or introducing short cuts in your home. Let your wife remain the mistress of the house and continue managing it as heretofore.

9th. Do not look for or demand special attentions from your wife just because you are home all day long. Do not expect her to cater to your whims and wishes all the time. Life is hard enough on her with you being around. Do not make it harder.

10th. Do not bring "idlers" or cronies to your home without your wife's knowledge and acceptance. It will be safer, easier and healthier for both of you.

11th. If you are acquiring a new hobby let it not be one that you follow at home or that places new chores and burdens on your wife.

12th. Find ways to show your regard and consideration for your wife's care and attentions in little ways. Show it by little, simple tokens of appreciation, by special courtesies, by chivalrous acts. She will "love" you for it and you will be repaid a hundredfold.

If you are the wife of a man who recently retired from work, who is "at sixes and sevens" and has not as yet adjusted himself to his enforced idleness, and if you want to make that transition period easier for him and for you, do it in these ways:

1st. Help your husband to adjust himself to his new status as a man out of work. He has been in harness for many years and for the time being feels out of place and out of sorts.

2nd. Let your husband have his way for a while even when he meddles in your affairs and is a terrific strain on you. You are the stronger and the smarter of the two. That phase will pass and before long he will find something else to do besides bothering you.

3rd. Do not nag at him or load household chores upon him. He is at loose ends for the time being. Perhaps he feels that he was forcibly put on the shelf or that old age has caught up with him or that he is no longer of any use to anyone. You have world-wide understanding. So—give him the courage and the sympathy he needs.

4th. Compromise on all matters, especially when he takes a stand on some minor detail. Let him feel that he is strong and masterful.

5th. Help him find new and appropriate interests and lead him into them without showing it. You know his likes, his good points and his weaknesses, and you can make it so much easier for him to become acclimated to his new life.

6th. Join him in some of his new activities even if you have to play-act. Make him feel that you are his pal, his best and closest friend. Pretend, make believe but be there, at his side . . .

7th. Praise him at every opportunity. Build up his ego. Make him feel that he means much to you. Plan the days ahead together and guide him in the planning, without seeming to do so and without encroaching upon his privacy.

Do these things one for the other. Be true helpmates one to the other, and the embers of your old love will glow anew as you continue on and on to better, brighter and happier days.

As a retired man, past 65, what can you do? A thousand and one different things. This great, big, wonderful world of ours is wide open to you and you have your choice to follow most any bent, interest or inclination. Make sure, however, to be good to yourself and keep in mind your age and your declining physical capacities, before you "go off the deep end" and take up something which may harm you and shorten your life.

Make no apologies for your age and do not be ashamed of the fact that you no longer have the physical prowess and stamina of twenty or thirty years back. What you lack in physical strength you gained in experience, in judgment, in maturity. What you lack in looks or youthful exuberance you gained in knowledge and understanding.

Lean more upon your mental capacities than upon physical endurance. If you were an all-around athlete before, you can now become a coach, a critic, a patron or a promoter. You can acquire an interest in arts, crafts, science or research. You can take pride and joy in cultivating people, in being useful or helpful to others, in doing things not for remuneration or rewards but for the pleasure it brings you, for the esthetic values, for the sense of personal satisfaction.

If you are looking for a hobby or a pastime select something in keeping with your age and possible future impairments. If you have no special interests or preferences, try your hand at several things. But, whatever they be, do not go at them as if your very life depended on it.

Take your time. Go at things calmly, leisurely. Follow only such activities which give you the desired relaxation, recreation or emotional outlet. Do not grow over-zealous and go overboard. Do only as much as you can handle with ease, comfort and with little or no exertion.

Do not feel disturbed or discouraged if your efforts do not bring immediate returns or recognition. Do not be disappointed if you cannot paint a masterpiece, compose a symphony, write a best seller or do something especially noticeable and spectacular. Look rather for the inner reward, for the sense of well-being, for the glow of personal satisfaction and accomplishment.

There are literally thousands of men and women, of all ages, and in all walks of life, who have never gained fame or fortune, who are hardly known outside of their immediate families and close circle of friends, who have led and are leading full, happy, glorious lives, replete with joy and satisfaction.

Do the things you want to do. You now have the time for it, even if it be only tending your roses, perfecting a gadget for home use, organizing a neighborhood baseball team or choral group, or just being a kind, thoughtful, helpful husband, neighbor or friend.

As a woman, past 65, what can you do? Numerous things, of course. But, first, reconcile yourself to the fact that you are no longer a "slick chick" to be whistled at. Accept your age gracefully. Do not go in for strenuous and often ludicrous efforts to hide your gray hair, your wrinkles, double chin or aging contours.

You can use many artifices, their number is limitless, and fool some of the people for a while, but you can never fool yourself, and your mental attitude is most important to your health and well-being. No woman can totally conceal her age. It will show up somewhere. If not in the face up-lift, the dyed hair or the tightly-laced figure, it will be noticeable in her neck, her hands, her eyes, her walk, talk or posture. Most people know where to look and how to recognize the tell-tale signs.

Some women, in their sixties or over, begin to act coy and kittenish. They wear daring clothes, smoke or drink with youthful abandon and make believe that they are young, beautiful and seductive. But beneath their make-believe mask is the constant fear that someone may catch them off guard and see them as they really are, and the price they pay for their pretense in trepidation and nervous tension is entirely too high.

A woman of age has her appeal, her loveliness, her value of appreciation and her place in the sun. She can find things to do and many ways to make life interesting and enjoyable. As in the case of the retired man, she can find joy and self-expression in many hobbies, pastimes, activities and leisure-time interests.

She can follow some of the arts, crafts and sciences, in the privacy of her home and with others as a member of a given group. Thus, she can satisfy her emotional needs and, if need be, sublimate her lack of male companionship.

Many exceptionally active and well coordinated groups consisting of and catering to the needs and interests of older people, the "senior citizens" as they are called, have been organized in all parts of the country within the last few years. They are sponsored by churches, fraternal organizations, social welfare and civic bodies as well as community centers, and offer many work and play opportunities to the older adults in the community.

In many states and cities the Adult Education Division of the City or County School System have special classes in gerontology, in public speaking, in history, in the arts and crafts and in many subjects of interest to senior citizens. If you do not know of any group in your city, call your local service clubs or various church organizations, the Community Council or the nearest Community Center, the Adult Education Department or the Parks and Recreation Departments of your city or county, and they will give you a list of the senior adult groups, who always welcome newcomers.

And so—if you are a retiree, with or without special training or abilities; if you are past 65 and free to do things, go out among the people in your city and join the group or groups which appeal to you. There among them, you will have many opportunities to be active, to find an outlet for your urges and energies and soon learn that you can add to the richness and the enjoyment of your life.

As a man or a woman past 65, the biggest problem you have to face is to find a purpose, an interest, that will keep your mind and your hands busy. You have to be doing something to make you feel that you are needed, wanted, useful and not a burden to yourself or to anyone else.

Age is not a matter of years even though you show the manifestations of older age. You are as old as your doubts and your fears, as your mental outlook and your activities.

As a matter of fact, and this may be a surprise to you, age has four dimensions. First, your calendar years; second, your feelings and emotions; third, your reaction to people and things around you; fourth, your thinking and your way of keeping yourself busy at something.

You cannot change your first dimension. It is there in your gray or white hair, in your glasses, in your hearing aid, in your dentures, in your weaker kidneys and in your inability to do many of the things you did in your younger years. But you can change and control the other three dimensions and through them remain young at heart, active in mind and effervescent in spirit.

You may be too old to take up strenuous sport activities, to start a new family or work steadily at some tiring job. But, you are never too old to acquire new interests, to learn new things, to make new friends, and to look for ways to add to the joys, beauty and pleasure of your daily living.

What are some of the ways in which you can do it? Here are twelve of them:

1. Accept your age and the natural impairments of your ad vanced years with grace and equanimity.

2. Adjust yourself to the inevitable changes in your physical status, in your stamina, and in your appearance, without fear, worry, apology or trepidation.

3. Remember that you are never too old to learn something

new, to change your attitudes, to acquire new and desirable habits or to make new friends.

4. If you can no longer follow some of the pursuits and pastimes you enjoyed in earlier years, find others in keeping with your age and its limitations. They may prove just as enjoyable, interesting and rewarding.

5. Your age or sex or bearing or position in life have nothing to do with your abilities to make new contacts and cultivate new friends.

6. Your mind retains its tremendous capacity to learn, to ab sorb, to accept and to remember. Put it to good use—now.

7. Make it your business to live this day to the full extent of your capacity to enjoy things, places and people.

8. Find ways to put your talents, experiences, background and past associations to work. Use them to teach and instruct others. Start a class at your church, your center, synagogue or club rooms, and whether it be youngsters or oldsters give them the benefit of what you know.

9. Cultivate a warm, friendly, cheerful attitude toward people in general and those with whom you come in contact day by day.

10. Seek understanding of yourself and closer communion with God, for you were created in His image and there is a spark of divinity in you.

11. Look for ways to express your creative urges, by joining classes in arts or crafts, in singing or dramatics, in writing or com posing. You may uncover hidden talents and gain many hours of joy and happiness.

12. Look for ways to do good, to help others, to be amiable, cooperative and support some worthwhile project in any way you can.

Put some of these ideas to work and then no matter how many more years you add to your age you will remain young, alert and happy.

The Twenty-seventh Hour

HOW TO GAIN AND RETAIN FRIENDS

WHY DO YOU LIKE one person and dislike another? On what do you base those likes and dislikes? Are they influenced by your concepts of beauty, intelligence, dependability, usefulness, helpfulness, conformity, amiability, make-up, friendliness or general behavior?

If your likes are based upon features, contours or beauty of form you have many points in your favor. Beauty has a tremendous appeal but its concepts and measuring standards vary from place to place, from person to person, and from nation to nation. For instance, among the Americans and the Anglo-Saxons feminine beauty was best exemplified by slimness of form and patrician features until recent years. Now, however, all attention is centered on ample bosoms and long, tapering limbs.

In Turkey, in Mexico and in many parts of South America it is heftiness and "fullness of beam" in the woman's form that is most admired. Among the Nigerians, the more brass rings a woman can put on her legs, from the ankle to the knee, the greater her feminine allure. Among the Ubangi it is the size and shape of her platter lips, while among other tribes it is the pierced nostrils, the elongated neck, the pointed head, the dangling ear lobes or the deliberately inflicted welts, scars and scabs on the face and on the body that makes the village belle irresistibly entrancing to the male. Tastes and likes certainly differ, for beauty is in the eyes of the beholder as witness the hundreds of plain, homely females who are loved, cherished and adored by their husbands.

If your likes are based upon appearance what tends to impress you most? Is it a person's build, posture, complexion or facial mien? Is it his walk, carriage, ready smile or the affability of manner? Is it his general neatness, his suave approach or chivalrous and romantic behavior?

Is it in the cut of his clothes and the way they are worn? Clothes do make a difference and play an important part in our initial and subsequent impressions. Women are slaves to fads and the dictates of fashion but men are as equally bound to antiquated customs and traditions, as witness the stiffened stand-up collar, the invariable tie and the cumbersome jacket, an absolute "must" in hot or cold weather, in men's street and business wear.

If your likes are based upon intelligence how do you determine the degree or the scope of knowledge? Does it have to be within fields related to your own interests or can it be of a general nature? If what impresses you most is general behavior how do you establish the standards to go by? Is it based upon your concepts of gentleness, kindness, tenderness, solicitude, readiness to follow your lead or the ability to make and maintain friendships?

Perhaps it is his personality that makes you like or dislike a given person? By personality is meant the impression you formed of his traits, attributes and make-up of character as shown by the way he talks and acts and responds to stimuli. Of course, a given personality can be assumed for a while. Most anyone can pretend to be what others expect him to be for a while, but such pretense is short-lived, and soon, perhaps too soon for the comfort of the pretender, the mask falls off and his true nature is revealed.

All of the foregoing leads to one conclusion. There are definite, tangible, recognizable reasons why you like or dislike a given person. Would you like to know what they are? Would you like to use such knowledge to evaluate yourself?

If so, take several sheets of paper and list on a separate sheet the things you like and dislike about a given person. Make up a number of sheets and then, considering each listing as a unit, use them to measure yourself. Compare the other fellow's traits, habits, mannerisms, characteristics, good and bad points with your own and let the comparisons tell their own story.

If you go about these analyses frankly and conscientiously, without alibiing, excusing or justifying your own shortcomings, you will have a fairly accurate guide as to what steps you have to take to acquire the qualities and attributes you prize in others.

However, the mere knowledge of what need be done is not enough. You may get people to accept you and manage to get by in life "as is" without much change in your character or personality but you will never get close to anyone and make or maintain desirable friendships.

The reasons may be obvious to you or need be stressed over and over again. Remember one important fact, friendships do not grow overnight. They have to be started, nurtured and cultivated. Their beginning is a seed planted in suitable soil which has to be watered, weeded and protected until it begins to bloom and even then it requires constant care and attention.

Friendship takes time to reach maturity. It is like a series of links in a chain, each link representing a given virtue, quality or attribute, and the chain is only as strong as its links.

Friendship cannot be bought or sold at any price or under any conditions. It cannot be traded, bartered for or transferred. True friendship like true love is one of God's rarest gifts and yet it is within the reach of everyone, because it is given gladly and freely to those who deserve it, at any time and all the time.

The first important step in building a lasting friendship is to make friends with yourself. Know your abilities and capacities, your failings and shortcomings, your qualities and attributes. Know what you can or cannot do and stay within your limitations.

If you have reached a given age and must watch out for certain things in your food, drink, play and activities do so faithfully, consistently. Do it without any omissions or reservations or else your physical well-being and your frame of mind will be affected, and that, in turn, will influence your contacts and relationships with others.

You cannot possibly be kind, sweet, thoughtful, helpful, considerate or friendly to anyone when you have a physical pain or discomfort. Likewise, you cannot possibly be amiable, sociable, hospitable, composed or level-headed when you are mentally disturbed or when your nerves are on edge and your temper is showing.

Friendship is a reciprocal process. You have to give before you can receive. No one will readily be your friend unless you have proven worthy of his trust, regard, confidence, esteem or affection. In other words, friendship has to be earned and that takes application, adaptation and cultivation.

Friendship starts with giving freely of one's self, with respect and consideration for the other person's rights and sensibilities, with common interchangeable interests. There has to be a bond of mutual understanding and that calls for certain qualities, attributes and mode of behavior.

What are some of the reasons that keep you from making friends and retaining their friendships? They may be due to many things and among them could be:

1. Your desire to punish others, and exact payment as it were, for the wrongs, privations and degradations you had to suffer in your youth and in your climb upward. For instance, if you are cold, callous, and totally indifferent to the pains, struggle and hardships of others as they are trying to gain a foothold you may be excusing your unwillingness to lend them a hand by saying: "I had to suffer and to struggle . . . I had to save, to scrimp, to blacken my face, to deny myself every joy and pleasure to get where I am . . . Why should I make it easy for someone else? Let him starve and slave as I did . . ." But back of it all is your ego.

2. Your desire to be "top dog", to direct, to dictate, to impose your will and whim, to throw your weight around, especially with those under you, regardless of the right or the wrong of it. That, too, is a self-centered attitude which can hardly build friends for you.

3. Your desire to build up your own importance by belittling or disparaging the value, the knowledge or the abilities of others, who may know as much or even more than you do and perhaps could add something to your own values and benefit.

4. Your desire to meet and to satisfy your own urges, wishes and desires, ahead of anyone else, with total disregard and indif ference for his rights, interests or sensibilities.

5. Your desire to mask your hatreds, hostilities, resentments,

disappointments or personal failures under the guise of love, duty, regard, affection, obligation, religious zeal, moral or ethical mores or an assumed righteousness.

6. Your tendency to deny recognition to others, to minimize their efforts or services, to sabotage their plans and thereby keep them from getting ahead of you.

7. Your tendency to be spiteful or belligerent, malicious or vindictive, and suspect without cause the aims, motives and actions of all those with whom you come in contact.

8. Your tendency to be surly, stubborn, intolerant or prejudiced, and totally unwilling to join others in a common task or to cooperate with them for the common good.

9. Your tendency to lose your temper, to become derisive, abusive or vituperative, because others do not follow your lead or dare to oppose you, in any way.

10. Your tendency to assume imperious airs or a superior attitude and insist that you know more or can do better or can never be wrong.

Any one of these desires or tendencies, singly or in conjunction with others can affect your relationship with others and keep you from making and keeping friends. Remember that the people around you are like a mirror. They reflect what they see. If you have no love or interest or friendship to show, the mirror will have nothing to reflect and the world around you will be blank.

What are some of the ways you can use to get along with people and make friends? Here are twenty-four of them listed arbitrarily. Their order of sequence is not indicative of their value or significance. It will be up to you to decide which come first and which are more important to you.

1. Do not assume an arrogant, officious, demanding, sarcastic, patronizing or supercilious attitude toward others at any time, under any excuse, pretext or provocation.

2. Be open-minded. Respect the beliefs, views and opinions of others, even if such do not coincide with your own ideas and conclusions.

3. Learn to keep your tongue in cheek and never speak ill of

anyone. Be especially careful not to spread rumors or be a "tattle-tale" when someone tells you something or confides in you.

4. Let your word be your bond. Never make a promise you cannot or do not intend to keep. Do not betray those who put their trust in you or deliberately lead them astray.

5. Do not be a zealot or a fanatic or go overboard on any plan, cause or ism and expect all others to follow you without fail. You may be wrong in your premises, beliefs or contentions and find yourself hanging high and dry on a limb.

6. Be slow to accuse, to censure or to condemn on general prin ciples or appearances. It is easy to misjudge, to misunderstand or misinterpret. It is easy to make assumptions or to jump to wrong conclusions and then find it difficult to pull back and make amends. Give the other fellow the benefit of the doubt and he will surely do the same for you.

7. Do not throw cold water on any plan or idea proposed by others just because it is not your own or because you do not like it. Listen to the reasons why it is being offered and evaluate them. It could be possible that you do not see those things in their proper light.

8. Do not "ride" those who are weaker than you or exact spe cial tributes from those under you, just because you are in a posi tion to throw your weight around. Times and conditions may change and the underdog may get to the top, and where will you be? It is seldom wise to antagonize people needlessly.

9. Be quick to praise people and speak well of a worthy project. Never miss the opportunity to say a kind word, to pat somebody on the back or to make someone feel better because you are nearby. In fact, encourage people to talk to you about themselves, about their hopes and problems. They will "love" you for it and flock to your side.

10. Do not deflate anyone's ego needlessly or deliberately. Let him have his moment of glory. It costs you nothing and takes nothing away from you. Puncturing his bubble may give you a kick, a satisfaction or a temporary advantage. But such tactics have a way to boomerang and in the long run you may be the heavy loser.

11. Be thoughtful and considerate. Think twice before you say or do something which may be harmful to anyone. And if you made a mistake apologize and try to make amends as soon as you can.

12. Do not curry favor with any one person or show open par tiality to him, in the presence of others. It may sit well with him but will hardly endear you to anyone else. Give your support to those worthy of it but temper it with consideration for the rights and feelings of others.

13. Be cautious in relying too much on glib promises. Do not pin all your hopes on strangers or fair-weather friends and expect them to go out of their way to please you or to help you. Let such things come to you as a surprise and you will have less heartache and get along much better and easier with others.

14. Do not take mere politeness, courtesy or curiosity as the open invitation to burden others with your woes, troubles or com plaints and expect them to sympathize with you at all times. You would not want to be placed in that embarrassing position and why should you expect it of others?

15. Be polite and courteous at all times, even to those who are rude, uncouth and offensive. It is amazing how rudeness wilts and bad manners retreat before calm gentility.

16. Do not confide too much in others or talk to them against a mutual friend or acquaintance. They may not share your views or find it impossible to keep your confidences. In either case your tales may "come home to roost" in the strangest garb and in the most embarrassing manner.

17. Be willing to listen to other points of view and invite criti cisms of your own. An exchange of opinions is often very helpful to crystallize a given plan or activity and gain the support needed to put it through.

18. Do not carry a chip on your shoulder and dare anyone to knock it off. Belligerence is an extremely poor invitation to friend ship. Furthermore, someone bigger and stronger than you may take the notion to knock your chip off and you may be on the losing end, much the worse for wear and tear.

19. Be ready to accept people at their face value and do not

look for or expect perfection in what they do or intend doing. It will be easier on them and on you and you will surely get along with people much better.

20. Do not demand or look for immediate returns for what you did or are doing for others. Let what you do come out of the goodness of your heart and let your deed be its own reward for the time being. The rest is sure to follow.

21. Be ready to admit that others can be as smart or alert, as good or efficient, as ingenious or resourceful as you are. Never underestimate the intelligence, the knowledge, the experience or the potentialities of those with whom you come in contact. Such attitude blocks all avenues to friendship.

22. Be quick to overlook minor failings or discrepancies com mitted in your presence, no matter how annoying they may be for the moment. Pass them off as lightly as you can. People will ap preciate it and be as considerate of your shortcomings.

23. Develop a kind, warm, sympathetic feeling toward people in general and those with whom you come in contact, in partic ular. It is the surest way to make friends.

24. Act toward others as you would want them to act toward you. In other words, practice the principles of the golden rule.

These are the twenty-four different ways to foster good will, to get along with people and to make friends. They do not represent all the things to do but it is safe to say that if you were to practice some of them consistently you would never be at a loss for friends.

The Twenty-eighth Hour

HOW TO CULTIVATE CHEERFULNESS

WHO IS THE PERSON you appreciate most, near you, when you are sad or depressed? Who is the one who gives you a "lift" and drives away your blues? He is not the richest, the handsomest, the cleverest or the closest friend you have but usually the one with a warm heart, with the ready smile and with the words that brighten and lighten your cares.

Cheerfulness is one of God's greatest gifts to man. It engenders hope, infuses courage and instills confidence. It is the sweetness of the spirit cultivated in the heart. It stifles despair and scatters gloom and despondency. There is an old belief that the stars dance at the birth and the angels rejoice in the coming of an habitually cheerful person.

The man who is always cheerful is never at a loss for friends, for social contacts or for activities to keep him young, alert and interested. No matter what his age, sex, physical appearance or station in life, he is as welcome as the flowers in May in any group or company. He seldom talks of his own troubles or takes time out to pity himself. He is always giving others a "lift", and in the midst of ministering to the troubles of others his own cares and worries dwindle and disappear.

The advice of the old, popular song, "Let a smile be your umbrella on a rainy, rainy day . . .", is as sound today as it ever was, because in the presence of a smile no dark clouds can ever linger and no gloom can ever last.

Cheerfulness generates laughter and through it we see the lighter, brighter, sunnier side of life. With laughter at your side you can always be assured a heart full of gladness and be most welcome anywhere and everywhere.

Cheerfulness is an acquired mental attitude and you can cultivate it in the privacy of your heart and within the limitations of your immediate environment. It is a frame of mind, a conscious deliberate effort to look for the bright side of things.

For instance, here is how one poet sees the thorn and the rose:

> I *have heard it said, since I was born,*
> *That every rose must have its thorn.*
> *No matter where it grows.*
> *It is true. This* I *can't deny,*
> *But it's also true, I do decry,*
> *That every thorn has its rose.*

There is a bright side, a good side, a cheerful note to everything around us, and many a so-called burden is in reality a boost, a help, a blessing. Schiller illustrated that concept in one of his poems, paraphrased as follows:

"When God created the birds of the world he gave them colorful plumage, sweet voices and hearts filled with cheer and song but no wings. He placed wing-like appendages upon the ground and said: "These shall be your joys or your burdens, your help or your handicaps. Carry them with you and use them as you wish . . ." The birds did not question the wisdom of God or feel disheartened. They lifted the appendages, kept them close to their little hearts and continued to sing joyously, cheerfully, as they hopped from place to place. Soon the appendages grew fast to their breasts and when spread out became pinions fair to carry the birds high into the air . . ."

You can generate cheerfulness within you in these ways:

1. Greet each morning with a smile and with cheery words as you meet your family, even if you have to pretend and play-act.

2. Carry your smile and the words that cheer with you far into the day as you go about your daily tasks.

3. Dwell upon bright, pleasant, cheerful and positive thoughts all through the day.

4. Radiate and reflect confidence and optimism all day long, no matter what the situation or the circumstance might be.

5. Refuse to rake up the sorrow of yesterday, borrow the prob abilities of tomorrow or magnify the burdens of today.

6. Do your best today. Live this day as justly, as fairly, as brightly as you can and avoid any and all excesses.

7. Refuse to be worried or allow yourself to be upset by triviali ties that could turn into irritations.

8. Steer clear of gloomy meditations or apprehensions. It is easy to find things to fret and fume about and be unhappy but why let them spoil a good day and a cheerful attitude?

9. Cultivate the habit of helping, encouraging and working with those less fortunate than you are. It is certain to increase your joys and pleasures.

10. Offer thanks to God and be grateful to Him for what you are, for what you have and for what you can enjoy today.

Take serious things lightly and when problems come your way meet them face to face with a stout heart, with a smile and with the will to go on. Life is not always smooth and easy and those of us who give up too quickly fall by the wayside, a burden to themselves and to all concerned.

Learn to laugh, and mirth and delight and cheerfulness will come your way to linger and to add meaning to your life. Here is how one poet put it:

> A *laugh is just like sunshine,*
> *It freshens all the day;*
> *It tips the peaks of life with light*
> *And drives the clouds away.*
> *The soul grows glad that hears it,*
> *And feels its courage strong.*
> *A laugh is just like sunshine*
> *To cheer the folks along.*
> *A laugh is just like music,*
> *It lingers in the heart;*
> *And where its melody is heard*
> *The ills of life depart.*
> *And happy thoughts come crowding*
> *Its joyful notes to greet.*
> *A laugh is just like music*
> *To make all life so sweet.*
> *A laugh is like a balm*
> *That soothes and eases pain;*
> *And where it's freely used*
> *Brings hope and cheer again.*
> *The man who keeps on laughing*
> *Will never go astray.*
> *His laugh will be his beacon*
> *That ever lights his way.*

Serenity has a close kinship with cheerfulness. The word comes from the Latin stem "serenus" and the suffix "ty", meaning the state of, or the quality of, being calm, serene. The synonyms are, calmness or evenness of temper, an unruffled manner, composure or tranquility, quietude or peacefulness.

Combine cheerfulness with serenity, as twin attributes, and you have the ideal personality. Such person is the one who has an air of competence, of poise, of dignity and self assurance about him. He is not easily perturbed or disturbed. He radiates peace and composure. He always takes the bright, optimistic point of view. He is sensible, level-headed and never lets emotion run away with him. He commands respect and recognition and is a welcome addition to any group or company, no matter how diverse their respective likes, interests or activities might be. For whatever the occasion or the circumstance he always carries with him a soothing, quieting, becalming and cheerful attitude.

The serene person utilizes and benefits by these virtues, and you, too, can acquire them. They are:

1st. Self-respect. It is in your refusal to violate the sacredness of being a creditable, exemplary human being and fall prey to the evils of lust, greed, passion or self-indulgence. It is in valuing your true promptings and inspirations as they arise. It is in the preservation of your own dignity and moral codes. It is in looking up to yourself and never doing anything of which you have to be afraid or ashamed, even in the privacy of your own heart. It is in being true to your conscience and your inner thoughts and never betraying the trust you place in your honor and integrity.

2nd. Self-reliance. It is in your ability to think for yourself and rely upon your judgment, in standing upon your own feet and carrying your share of duties and obligations as they come your way. It is in your willingness to do all you can in helping yourself before asking, expecting or demanding that others help you. It is in your readiness to accept your responsibilities to yourself and to those who put their trust in you.

3rd. Self-discipline. It is in your ability to hold your feelings and emotions in check and never allowing them to master you. It is in learning to control those urges, promptings and desires which are not worthy of you as a normal, sensible human being and which are inimical to desirable, amiable and peaceful relationships with others.

4th. Self-confidence. This implies belief not only in yourself, in your own innate goodness, but also in your fellow men and in the wisdom of God. You must believe in yourself first or else you have no basis for any belief. In so far as you are concerned, you are the originator of all thought, the instigator of all action, the master of your own little world. Figuratively speaking, nothing can reach you, affect you, hurt you, impress you or upset you, because it has to come to you through your own sense channels, through your own feelings and emotions, and you can modify, simplify or nullify it to suit you.

Believe in others and cultivate a warm, friendly feeling toward people in general and toward those with whom you associate, in particular. No one can be an island unto himself. In our modern social order you have to come in contact with all types of people and unless you learn to accept them and adjust yourself to being part of the existing order you will be most miserable and unhappy. In spite of all you see, read or hear the average man is honest, fair-minded, conscientious, helpful and law-abiding. Keep that in mind and do not set yourself up as a censor, mentor or arbitrator.

Believe in God. He is the Lord of the universe, our Father in Heaven, the fountainhead of all life. Put your trust in Him and He will guard you and protect you. Turn to Him in your hour of need with an abiding faith and He will not forsake you.

5th. Peace with yourself. If there is one thing that will help you gain serenity and equanimity it is being at peace with yourself and fighting lust, avarice, envy, suspicion, anger and false pride, the sworn enemies of peace within you. Peace with yourself is in cultivating your better qualities, in developing desirable habits, in maintaining amicable relationships with your fellow men and in refusing to become incensed and upset by occasional slips in our contacts with others. Peace with yourself lies in looking for and in finding satisfaction and contentment in the simple, little pleasures at hand and in making the most of everyone of them.

These are some of the virtues which help us achieve personal serenity and make life richer, sweeter and brighter for us.

These may have been the thoughts and the sentiments that prompted the writing of the immortal poem, "Waiting", by John Burroughs:

> *Serene, I fold my hands and wait,*
> *Nor care for wind nor tide nor sea;*
> *I rave no more 'gainst time or fate,*
> *For lo! My own shall come to me.*
>
> *I stay my haste, I make delays;*
> *For what avails this eager pace?*
> *I stand amid the eternal ways*
> *And what is mine shall know my face.*
>
> *Asleep, awake, by night or day*
> *The friends I seek are seeking me;*
> *No wind can drive my bark astray*
> *Nor change the tide of destiny.*
>
> *What matter if I stand alone?*
> *I wait with joy the coming years;*
> *My heart shall reap where it has sown,*
> *And garner up the fruits of tears.*
>
> *The waters know their own, and draw*
> *The brook that springs in yonder heights;*
> *So flows the good with equal law*
> *Unto the soul of pure delights.*
>
> *The stars come nightly in the sky,*
> *The tidal wave unto the sea;*
> *No time or space, no deep nor high,*
> *Can keep my own away from me.*

Is this not a beautiful concept of serenity? Would you be willing to accept it as your own and let it become part of your cheerful attitude toward life and conditions and people around you?

Make this concept your very own. Let it add to your peace of mind, to your joys of living, as you go steadily onward and upward on your private stairway to success and happiness, only two space hours away.

The Twenty-ninth Hour

HOW TO LOOK FOR HAPPINESS

PERHAPS one of the reasons why you do not enjoy happiness may lie in the fact that you never defined its concept in your mind. This is not at all unusual because were you to ask a dozen people, at random, as to what would make them happy you would have a dozen different answers.

Among them would be love, money, friends, marriage, health, good looks, fame, children, power, prosperity, a good job, a nice home, a family, a business, popularity, public acclaim or the ability to loaf and do as they please.

All of these things contribute to one's measure of happiness but not one of them can truly fill the bill because they are not an assurance of serenity, tranquility, contentment or inner satisfaction that are synonymous with happiness.

Our poets, thinkers and philosophers have their definitions. Joseph Addison believed that happiness is enjoyment of one's self and the loyalty of select friends. Hume claimed that happiness is a propensity for joy, hope, gaiety and cheerfulness. Thomson maintained that true happiness consisted of doing good while Antonius contended that happiness is no other than soundness and perfection of mind.

Happiness is joy wherever we find it, and perhaps this story, often related before, may interest you.

A Phoenician King suddenly developed the fear that he would be forcibly dethroned and turned into a beggar. Held in the grip of his growing fear he lost his appetite, developed insomnia, grew irritable, began to abuse his wives and advisors and threatened to behead every member of his court.

Fearful of their lives they held several secret meetings and then implored the High Priest to Astarte to seek guidance from her. He prostrated himself seven times seven before her altar, intoned the seven mystic incantations, took seven sips of the sacrificial wine and fell into a sleep. He dreamed a strange dream, hurried back to the palace later and told the King that a sure cure for his illness would be to wear the shirt of a truly happy man.

And so, a proclamation was issued and messengers were sent forth into every part of the land, from Tyre to Sidon, to Utica, to Carthage and along the shores of the Mediterranean. At last in one of the obscure market places a beggar was found who was said to be the most cheerful and happiest man alive.

He was taken to the King's palace and there amidst the glitter and the opulence of the court he was promised honors and riches in exchange for his shirt, but the beggar refused all the offers. The King grew angry. He ordered that the beggar be stripped of his clothes and then be flogged to death. The guards tore off the beggar's tattered cloak but to everybody's amazement he had no shirt . . .

Apparently the beggar needed no shirt to be happy. But what about you? What would make *you* happy? Do you believe that fame, fortune or acclaim would bring you happiness? If this were so, the rich and powerful and famous among us would be the happiest people alive. But judging by frequent newspaper accounts of strife, trouble, tension and difficulty among them all is not well with the so-called fortunate ones.

There must be other ways to gain peace, joy, happiness and contentment. We see it in the faces and the actions of healthy, active children. We find it among the poor and simple folk who lead uneventful and unpretentious lives. We notice it among the deeply religious who gain strength and serenity in their abiding faith. We witness it among the old who have learned to accept life as it is and live one day at a time.

Happiness can be achieved in all walks of life and under every conceivable type of circumstance and environment. It is a way of life, a simple mixture of adaptation, application and cultivation. Perhaps this story, adapted from an old sermon, may give you a new concept of happiness and start you on your way.

When God decided to grant the gift of happiness to man he called the angels together, handed them a tiny capsule and said: "I placed the seeds of happiness within this capsule and you are to determine how man shall find them, plant them and reap the ensuing rewards. The buds will be fragile at first but when properly cared for they will sprout into hardy plants and give luscious fruit through the years. Be sure to place the capsule within easy reach of every deserving person but far from greedy, grasping fingers, so that only those worthy of my trust shall enjoy the fruits of happiness."

Among the suggestions made were: 1. To put the seeds in the waters which man drinks. 2. To place them in the foods he eats. 3. To let them float in the air he breathes. 4. To sift them in the ground upon which he walks. 5. To link them with his daily contacts. 6. To tie them in with the joys and carefree laughter of his children. 7. To instill them into man's dreams and aspirations. But objections were raised to every suggestion until one angel proposed that the capsule of seeds be placed in the innermost corner of man's heart.

The idea found favor with God and so it was decreed. From that day on, an angel comes to all of us, moments before our birth, and implants within a corner of our heart the capsule of seeds. It remains there throughout our entire life and at any time we earnestly desire it we can germinate the seeds, watch them grow into blooming plants and enjoy the fruits of happiness.

To make things easier for you there is no set method of cultivation. You need no special talents or aptitudes or any particular prerequisites. It is a matter of your choice and your preferences. You can plant the seeds and have them germinate for you in these ways:

1st. Recognize your limitations. Do not undertake any task or responsibility beyond your means or your abilities to handle it. If you have certain handicaps and cannot change them learn to live with them and triumph over those disabilities. Sarah Bernhardt with her broken leg, Lionel Barrymore crippled with arthritis and Franklin D. Roosevelt incapacitated with polio, to mention only three of them, managed to get their share of happiness, in spite of their torturing physical disabilities.

2nd. Evaluate your good qualities which differentiate you from others and utilize them to the best advantage. Capitalize upon the things you can do best. Refuse to be a poor imitation of someone else. Be true to yourself and do the most you can with what you have.

3rd. Stop being jealous, envious or covetous. They breed suspicion, intolerance and misunderstanding. They engender the feeling that people want to harm you or belittle you and may lead you to "do unto them before they do unto you". And that is sure to lead to unpleasant relations, to hostile feelings and to unhappiness.

4th. Stop surmising, conjecturing or jumping to wrong conclusions. That mental attitude breeds numerous counterparts. It brings out the worst in us and in others. It leads to estrangements and quickly converts friends into enemies.

5th. Ignore petty annoyances and trivial indiscretions. Try to pass them off as unobtrusively as you can. It is so easy to let ourselves be poisoned by anger, spite, foolish pride or a sense of assumed indignation. Life holds enough trials and tribulations without the need to magnify little slights or non-intentional hurts. People are naturally selfish, forgetful, self-centered, indifferent and ungrateful. Recognize those common failings and make allowances for them. Thus, the less you will expect or demand from others, the fewer your disappointments and the greater your pleasure when people do something for you, totally unexpected.

6th. Count your blessings and rejoice in what you have. Focus your attention upon the riches you possess, in the full use of your senses, in your healthy body, in your sound mind, in your family, in the work you enjoy doing, in your circle of friends, and in all the things you prize and cherish. No amount of money would entice you to sacrifice any of it and thus you are rich beyond measure.

7th. Cultivate the sincerity of prayer and the uplifting surge of abiding faith. Faith is the substance of all the things we hope for and more things are wrought by prayer than we can dream of. Faith is the pencil of the soul, prayer is the gateway to Heaven. Faith lifts us above all fear, prayer is the peace of the spirit. So— have faith in God and when you are troubled do not hesitate to pray, for it is sure to bring you a measure of peace and happiness.

8th. Be quick with your smile and mix the milk of human kindness with everything you do, by day or by night, at home, at work or at play. Nothing lightens or brightens our tasks as quickly and as easily or tends to make our contacts with others more pleasant. It is one of the surest ways to generate a feeling of good will and enjoy the fruits of happiness.

9th. Cultivate a point of view and an attitude of mind that sees the good rather than the bad, the beautiful rather than the ugly sidè7the advantages rather than the disadvantages, the things to be pleased about rather than those which tend to displease. Then, no matter what the condition or the circumstance, you will derive a greater measure of satisfaction and happiness.

10th. Look for ways to enjoy the simple, ordinary, normal happenings of the day. If you had a good night's sleep, ate a well-cooked, well served meal or chatted amiably with some friend for a while, be glad of it. If you had a pleasant day at work or at home, took part in some enjoyable activity or found pleasure at someone's home, be glad of it. If you bought something at bargain, bested a friend at some social game or won one of the prizes at a bazaar, be glad of it. Put those glad moments side by side or put them one atop another, and they will surely add to your happiness.

11th. Practice self-control and self-discipline. Of course, it is nice to get angry at times, to lose one's temper, to accuse or to criticize, to "tell off" somebody. It gives you a sense of importance. It brings a feeling of relief, of justification or vindication. But it cannot build friendship or amicable relationship, and a fence once broken cannot be mended so easily. Yield ground now and then. If you were wrong you saved yourself needless trouble or resentments later; if you were right, people will eventually see things your way.

12th. Look for happiness within yourself. The seeds are there and only you can give them life and growth. Do it by keeping busy at the things you like or learned to like. Do it by keeping an open mind to suggestions, criticisms and differences in viewpoints. Do it by avoiding excesses of any kind that may be harmful to your physical or nervous system. Do it by maintaining a kindly feeling toward all with whom you come in contact.

Then, no matter what you do, where you go or what your station in life might be, you will be germinating your seeds of happiness and enjoy its fruits through the days yet to come.

The Thirtieth Hour

HOW TO GENERATE SPIRITUAL BELIEF

WHAT IS THE SECRET SOURCE of strength within you that engenders hope, promotes courage, fosters the desire and instills the determination to reach upward into the nobility of thought? What is the inner urge that spurs you on and on to seek higher spiritual values?

It is in self-dedication based on belief. But what is belief? The dictionary defines it as an acceptance of true or assumed facts, as a mental affirmation of what appears to us to be true and trustworthy.

Belief is an act of mind. It is generated by reasoning, by prevailing customs, by established practices, by credence, by prejudice, by authoritative assurance, by persuasive repetitions, or by the personal desire to accept willingly that which we wish to be true. Belief is faith, trust, conviction, reliance, assurance.

Some of us wear our beliefs like garments that we put on and take off to suit the purpose or the occasion. However we fail to gauge correctly the time or the place and often use the wrong garment, to our distinct loss and discomfort.

Belief is like an infusion. It is the universal reagent that colors, filters, modifies or amplifies every situation and thereby affects our feelings, actions and reactions. F. W. Robertson rightly said: "To believe is to be happy and strong, for only as we believe fully can we act cheerfully and do anything worth doing."

Have a belief in which you can put your trust, your heart and soul. Believe in yourself, believe in the innate fairness of man and, above all, believe in God. Let your belief generate faith. It is the substance of all things hoped for and none can live as serenely and as pleasantly as those who live by faith.

Faith is a habit which grows stronger as we live more and more by it. True faith accepts God without reservations and places all trust and confidence in Him. No other blessing bestowed on man can be more useful or desirable or more conducive to inner peace and happiness than a firm, unshakable religious belief in the goodness, the greatness, the righteousness and the loving-kindness of God.

Religious faith is a God-given gift. It is yours to hold and to benefit by. It is the key that unlocks God's treasures to us. It is the ever-present urge to reach upward. It is the absolute confidence in God as the Father, the Creator, the Preserver, and such faith is continually renewed and reactivated by prayer.

The innate goodness and nobility of man is exemplified by some of his prayers. Here are paraphrased excerpts of two such prayers which you may find helpful and inspiring.

The first, from the "Optimist's Prayer" by William Robinson: "Oh! Unseen power that rules the destinies of the children of earth, teach me the symphony of life. Reveal to me the joy of being loving, charitable and self-sacrificing. Teach me to play life's game with courage and confidence. Endow me with wisdom to guard my tongue and my temper. Enable me to give a smile instead of a frown and a cheery, kindly word instead of harshness or bitterness. Make me sympathetic in the face of sorrow. When I am wounded pour into my wounds the balm of hope. Imbue me with courage undaunted to rise and continue in the midst of strife. Keep me humble in every revelation of life, meek in success and uplifted in sorrow. Grant me, Oh Lord, that I may be a true and loyal friend."

The second, from the "Actor's Prayer" by Dr. Frank Crane: "Oh God, Thou art my secret, the great spirit that stands silently by. Let me triumph inwardly and taste the joy of Thy friendship. Wash my heart clean. Give me the holy ambition to do my tasks well. Teach me ways to resist despair, to master my passions and to heal unworthy weaknesses. Reveal to me the satisfaction of virtue, the inner rewards of loyalty, of helpfulness and of self-control. Let me touch the infinite and share the divine current that thrills all high souls. Save me from the bogs of pettiness, from egotism, envy, self-pity and all the corrosives that mar life. God of my soul, help me to be a man . . ."

And here is one more stirring expression of abiding spiritual faith, written by Caroline Mason and entitled "At Eventide":

At cool of day with God I walk
My garden's grateful shade;
I hear His voice among the trees
And I am not afraid.
I see His presence in the night,
And though my heart is awed,
I do not quail beneath the sight
Or the nearness of my God.
He speaks to me in every breeze,
He smiles from every star;
He is not deaf to me, nor blind,
Nor absent, nor afar.
His hand that shuts flowers to sleep,
Each in its dewy fold,
Is strong my feeble life to keep
And competent to hold.
I cannot walk in darkness long,
His light is by my side;
I cannot stumble or go wrong

While following such guide.
He is my star and my defence,
How shall I fail or fall?
My helper is Omnipotence!
My ruler ruleth all!
The powers below and the powers above
Are subject to His care;
I cannot wander from His love,
Who loves me everywhere.
Thus dowered and guarded with Him
I walk this peaceful shade;
I hear His voice among the trees
And I am glad and not afraid.

How steadfast such spiritual belief and abiding faith must be! How serene and peaceful in the midst of daily doubt and strife!

You, too, can acquire the same staunch belief, the same abiding faith, expressed so beautifully in the poem and the two prayers quoted. But first, you must establish in your mind your concept of a supreme being and crystallize your feelings about the power of prayer.

Perhaps you have been taking yourself and the world around you for granted, without any thought or concern about what makes it work. But, can you possibly behold the wonders of animate and inanimate life around you and not feel something deep inside?

Can you look at the sun, the moon, the sky studded with stars, at the oceans deep, the mountains high, the deserts dry, the forest and the rivers teeming with life, without seeing in it all the hand of a supreme, divine power?

Can you envision the thousands of nebulae and the numerous other worlds up in the sky, millions of miles apart, whirling at speeds that would carry them around the earth in a few minutes and yet taking many light years in racing through the infinity of space to reach your eyes, without seeing in them the hand of a supreme being?

Can you think of yourself as the most complex living organism known, being the highest form of life on earth, and visualize within you other forms of life, so small that they can be seen only through a powerful microscope, all of you pulsating with life, all of you going through the same cycle of birth and growth and death, without seeing in it the hand of some omniscient, omnipotent power?

How would you account for it all? What is your concept of this supreme power? How would you describe it, in the light of your adult reasoning and understanding? Perhaps you would do well to turn first to the writings of our poets, thinkers, philosophers and spiritual leaders.

Goethe said in part: "As a man is, so is his God . . ." He implied that our concept of God is as big as our belief and understanding. Cowper said: "Happy the man who sees God employed in all the good and ill that checquers life . . ."

You may prefer the words of Lowell: "Be He nowhere, God is in all that liberates and lifts, in all that humbles, sweetens and consoles . . ." Or, you may like Richter's concept: "God is the light which never sees itself, makes all things bright and visible and clothes itself in colors . . ." Or, you may be more inclined to follow Moore, who penned these lines:

Thou art, O God, the life and light
Of all this wondrous world we see;
Its glow by day, its smile by night,
Are all but reflections caught from Thee.
Where'er we turn Thy glories shine
And all things fair and bright are Thine!

Bishop Heber's concept is very striking, for he says of God:

There is an Eye that never sleeps
Beneath the wing of night;
There is an Ear that never shuts
When sinks the beam of light.
There is an Arm that never tires
When human strength gives way;
There is a Love that never fails

When earthly loves decay.
The Eye is fixed on seraph throngs,
The Ear is filled with angels' song,
The Arm upholds the worlds on high.
That love is thron'd beyond the sky.

Perhaps one of the finest concepts of God are these excerpts, taken from Rabbi Joshua Liebman's book, "Peace of Mind".

"God is all good but he does not abrogate the moral laws of life for anyone . . . He established set laws in the universe and he expects them to operate as such . . . He has given you a mind and a conscience and he expects you to use them ... He has given you the ability to distinguish between right and wrong and he expects you to follow the right precepts ... If you abuse yourself or trespass nature's simple laws he will not set his world topsyturvy just to rescue you from the consequences of your deeds . . . Do not expect him to be wheedled into violating the principles of life just to please you . . ."

Liebman continues: "There are no favorites among his children ... no partiality in his universe . . . Man must help himself first . . . God's abilities are limited by the very nature of the world he created . . . God is not a magician who can change to your liking just because you ask for it . . ."

And here is the last excerpt we will use. It is from the pen of Mordecai Kaplan: "God is the Oneness that spans the fathomless deeps of space and the measureless eons of time . . . God is the unity of all that is ... God is the mystery of life, the creative flame that transfigures lifeless substances . . . God is the faith by which we overcome the fear of loneliness, of helplessness, of failure and of death . . . God is in the hope which cleaves the dark abysms of sin, of suffering and of despair . . . God is in the love which creates, protects and forgives . . ."

How can you serve God? How can you worship him best? Lucius Seneca, the philosopher who lived nearly two thousand years ago, may have had the right idea when he wrote: "God wants no sacrifices of life and blood, for what pleasure can He have in the slaughter of the innocent . . . Worship Him with a pure heart and a good honest purpose . . . God wants no temples to be built to Him, of stone and marble piled on high, but to be consecrated in the heart of every man . . ."

Take these concepts and expressions to heart and when you find yourself filled with doubt, fear, weariness or trepidation, turn to God. Call to him from the innermost depths of your being and He will come to you. Talk to God by day or by night. Confide in Him and tell Him of your troubles. Bare your heart to Him and seek His help with a simple, sincere prayer.

God is everywhere. He is infinitely good, kind, just, merciful and righteous. He dwells within your heart and you can reach Him there, at any time and all the time. Have faith in Him and He will never let you down.

Pray to God and benefit by the wonder-working power of prayer. It need not be couched in pious, lofty, virtuous words, in prescribed language or in authorized prayer-book form. Make up your prayer as you go along. Make it as plain, simple and direct as you wish. Talk to God as if He were there beside you. Talk to Him as openly and as readily as you would to your closest and dearest friend.

Your prayer need not be made in a church, a temple, a chapel or in a synagogue. You may pray whenever the urge comes or whenever the need arises or wherever you may be at the moment, and it will be fully acceptable in the eyes of God. You can voice your prayer or keep the words in. It does not matter to God, for if the prayer comes from your heart He will hear every word of it.

Sincere heartfelt prayer exercises a deep, profound spiritual influence upon us. When we pray for material things for ourselves we find it completely dissatisfying because the selfish motive is there. But when we pray for others and show interest and concern in them our own troubles seem to be lightened and our prayers find favor in the eyes of God.

Our prayer in behalf of others gives us strength and confidence. It induces kindness, promotes thoughtfulness and engenders consideration. It fosters friendship, begets benevolence, adds to our well-being and brings us nearer to God.

"Do not be afraid to pray," says Coleridge, "to pray is right.

Pray in the darkness, if there is no light. Pray, if you can, with hope, but pray, though hope be weak and sick with delay".

Prayer is the direct bell to God. To paraphrase the words of C. M. Spurgeon: "Prayer pulls the rope below and the giant bell rings above in the ears of God. Some people scarcely stir the bell, their prayers are so languid; others give only an occasional pluck of the rope. But he who wins with heaven is the man who prays often and with his heart. It is he who grasps the rope openly, boldly, and pulls continuously at it with all his might . . ."

Would you like to sleep soundly through the coming night and awake in the morning fully alive and refreshed? Then try this formula. When you retire tonight, shut out all noises, relax, close your eyes and think of all the good things that happened to you during the day just passed. Recall the nice words said to you, the good deeds you did for others and all the happy incidents of the day, and as you go over them, one by one, offer a prayer of thanks to God. Do it again the next night and on the night following and soon sound, refreshing sleep will be yours.

Can you recall the days when you, as a child, used to run to your mother to have her "kiss away" your tears, your fears and your hurts. Her kiss had the magic touch. It did wonders for you. Why? Because in your eyes your mother was your tower of strength, your protector, your haven of security. Her kiss and her embrace, her concern and tender words, were your assurance of love, of sympathy and of understanding. You knew once again that mother would be there as ever before to comfort you, to shield you and protect you from harm. Her kiss was the token of her presence. It dried your tears, eased your pain and dissipated your fears.

You can turn to God with the same faith, belief and assurance, and He will be your tower of strength, your haven of refuge and security. You can build a chapel to Him within your breast, with you as the priest, your heart as your offering and the ground you walk on as your altar.

Jeremy Taylor expressed that thought in these words: "You build your own road to God and no one can hinder your privacy, for prayer is the sure way to Him. It is the peace of your spirit, the stillness of your thought, the evenness of recollection, the seat of meditation, the rest of your cares and the calm of your tempest." Give room to those inner urges to pray. Let them help you benefit by their wonder-working power and the stimulating, energizing, uplifting magic of spiritual belief. They will become your "beacon of light" to steer you through the rip-tides of trouble, and your "rock of ages" to give you the strength, the hope, the courage, the faith you need to hold on and weather the storms of life.

The Final Word

THE NEW LOOK

THERE YOU ARE! At the end of your reach into time and space to find success and happiness . . .

You completed the thirty day climb, your thirty hour projection into time and space, into the limitless heights of personal achievement, and have reached the top of your private stairway to success and happiness. You can now look back and look down, from the uppermost balcony, with safety and assurance, and see with justifiable pride how much of the old and the undesirable you left below.

If you climbed one riser at a time, as suggested, you are well adjusted now to the new look and the new heights around you. The great, big, wide, wonderful world is more beautiful than ever and there are so many things you can do now to add to your joys and pleasures.

You are to be congratulated for having maintained the proper sequences in climbing upward, for having followed through conscientiously on the suggestions given and for keeping faith with yourself throughout those thirty days.

You may still be in the same surroundings, be still limited by your age or economic status and restricted by the old environment.

But you made important and far-reaching changes within yourself, in your make-up, in your mental attitude, in your relationships with others, and you are no longer bound by the old restrictions and limitations.

You are no longer the same individual who started thirty days ago, when you mounted your first stair on your thirty steps to happiness. You left most of the old "self" far below. You formed new habits, gained in self-understanding and learned how to live better with yourself and with others. You know now how to gen erate cheerfulness within yourself, how to make friends and how to add to your enjoyments.

You are well on your way to better and happier days, but be ever on your guard against the return and the encroachment of old habits. In the light of your age, thirty days is too short a time to throw off and to eliminate all the old, non-desirable trends and tendencies. One sure way to guard against them is to go back and review those steps in this book which apply specifically to you.

Each time you review such steps and follow through on the ideas and suggestions given they will be just as effectual as before. Each repetition will do as much good and help you to disable, to disrupt and to deliberate the effort of old habits to reassert themselves. Each conscious, deliberate opposition will weaken your old habits and lower their tendency to return.

Make it a daily ritual to go back to those steps, in whole or in part, which you underlined previously for special review and attention. Go over them again and again until they become an integral part of your habitual pattern of behavior. Then, you will be able to retain the new heights you have reached, benefit in full by your new look, and glory in your accomplishments.

However, should you find yourself slipping back unwillingly into some of the old habits, offset them in this way. Let us assume that one of those habits is procrastination. You can never get started on something you want to do or ought to do. You keep putting it off from day to day, from week to week, without any real reason behind it, other than inaction, inactivity, reluctance or simple procrastination.

Well, when you go to bed tonight, relax as completely as you can, let your mind go back to the thing you have been procrastinating, and say to yourself, aloud, in the privacy of your room. "There is no reason why I should delay it any longer ... I will start doing it tomorrow ... I will start doing it tomorrow . . . I ... will . . . start . . . doing ... it ... tomorrow . . ." Keep repeating the same phrase aloud, over and over again, until you drop off to sleep.

This is a form of controlled auto-suggestion. It is a conscious, deliberately given verbal order to your thalamus to take desirable action. It is the last impression made intentionally by you upon your sensitized mental screen and it will linger on and on during your sleeping hours.

Then next morning or sometime during that day you will feel more inclined to start the job, the task or the activity you have been postponing all the while. Of course, if your habit of procrastination is well entrenched you may not be able to throw it off with one auto-suggestion procedure. You may have to repeat the routine of giving verbal directions to your thalamus just before you fall asleep a number of times.

But, whatever be the times needed, do it over and over again. Give yourself last-minute instructions, spoken aloud, to throw off the shackles of the procrastination habit. Let those mobilized, verbalized, energized auto-suggestions assert themselves and they will surely take over and displace the old habit.

Time and nature are in your favor, and the same routine can be followed in discarding and replacing any habit you wish to displace. It is within your power. So—give yourself the chance. Remain steadfast in your purpose to retain your new look, your new status, your new self. And may God, the all-powerful, the all-merciful, be with you and guard you on this day and all your happy days yet to come.